매일
10분 영어

이현석의 정면돌파 스피킹

여가생활편 Unit 66 - 150

집필 및 진행 **이현석**

EBS
www.ebse.co.kr

Prologue

영어의 핵심 음운현상을 선별 적용하여 발음과 강세 훈련을 하는 정면돌파 스피킹에 많은 성원을 보내주셔서 감사합니다. 많은 분들이 자신의 영어 발음에 더욱더 자신감을 갖는 계기가 되었다고 말씀해 주셨습니다.

발음과 강세 원리를 다룬 1권에 이어서 출간되는 이번 2권에서는 다양한 여가 생활 전반의 17개의 주제를 담아 보았습니다. 가장 먼저, 우리가 즐겨 보고 듣는 영화, 음악, 방송, 스포츠에서는 가장 중요한 주제 관련 표현들을 정리해보고, 정확한 발음과 강세를 훈련하는 연습을 해볼까 합니다.

예를 들어, 한 영화 작품이 흥행에 성공을 했다는 말을 box office라는 단어를 이용해서 만들어보고, 합성어의 강세 규칙에

맞게, 앞 단어에 강세 주는 연습을 할 예정입니다. 무엇보다 영어 말하기는 실생활에 바로 쓸 수 있는 주제와 표현들로 연습을 하는 것이 가장 좋습니다. 그래야 활용을 해보게 되고, 학습 동기가 올라갑니다.

이번 정면돌파 2권에 수록된 주제들과 함께 우리 실생활 주제들에 대한 표현력을 늘려보고, 우리의 영어 전달력을 크게 향상시키는 계기가 되었으면 합니다.

이현석 드림

Contents

노란색 강세 (단어 강세이든, 문장 강세이든 노란색으로 통일)
볼드체 테마별 주요 표현의 가독성을 높이기 위한 강조 표시

composition

테마별 대화문 85강으로 구성하여
핵심단어의 발음과 강세를 먼저 익힌다.

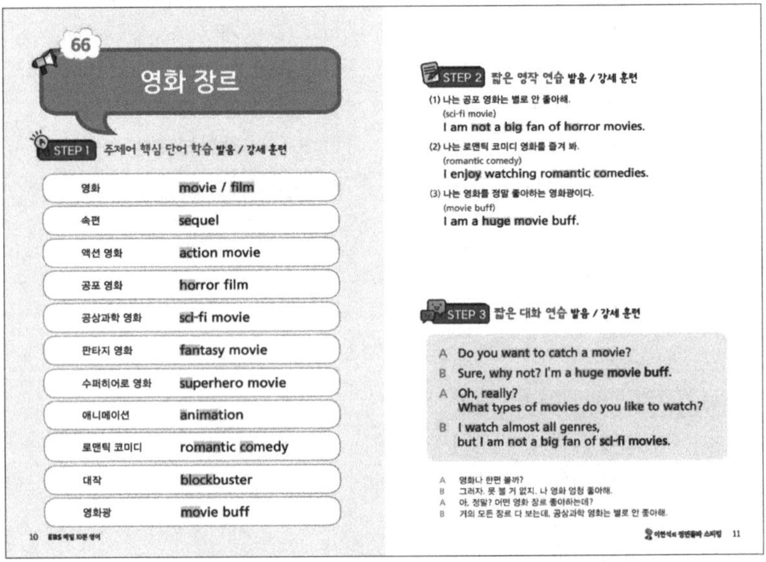

66

영화 장르

STEP 1 주제어 핵심 단어 학습 발음 / 강세 훈련

영화	movie / film
속편	sequel
액션 영화	action movie
공포 영화	horror film
공상과학 영화	sci-fi movie
판타지 영화	fantasy movie
수퍼히어로 영화	superhero movie
애니메이션	animation
로맨틱 코미디	romantic comedy
대작	blockbuster
영화광	movie buff

10 EBS 매일 10분 영어

STEP 2 짧은 영작 연습 발음 / 강세 훈련

(1) 나는 공포 영화는 별로 안 좋아해.
(sci-fi movie)
I am not a big fan of horror movies.

(2) 나는 로맨틱 코미디 영화를 즐겨 봐.
(romantic comedy)
I enjoy watching romantic comedies.

(3) 나는 영화를 정말 좋아하는 영화광이다.
(movie buff)
I am a huge movie buff.

STEP 3 짧은 대화 연습 발음 / 강세 훈련

A Do you want to catch a movie?
B Sure, why not? I'm a huge movie buff.
A Oh, really?
What types of movies do you like to watch?
B I watch almost all genres,
but I am not a big fan of sci-fi movies.

A 영화나 한편 볼까?
B 그러자. 못 볼 거 없지. 나 영화 엄청 좋아해.
A 아, 정말? 어떤 영화 장르 좋아하는데?
B 거의 모든 장르 다 보는데, 공상과학 영화는 별로 안 좋아해.

이현석의 정면돌파 스피킹 11

짧은 문장의 영작과 짧은 대화 연습을 하면서
발음과 강세를 연습한다.

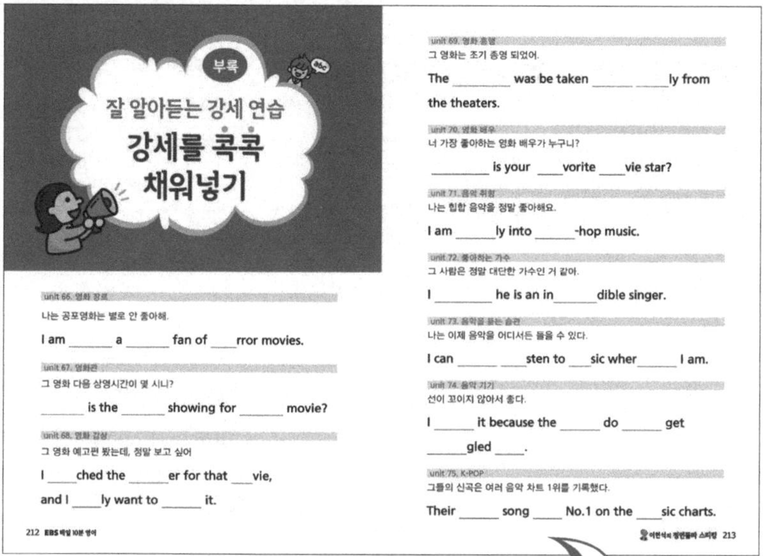

부록

잘 알아듣는 강세 연습

강세를 콕콕 채워넣기

unit 66. 영화 장르

나는 공포영화는 별로 안 좋아해.

I am ______ a ______ fan of ___rror movies.

unit 67. 영화관

그 영화 다음 상영시간이 몇 시니?

______ is the ______ showing for ______ movie?

unit 68. 영화 감상

그 영화 예고편 봤는데, 정말 보고 싶어

I ____ched the ______er for that ___vie,

and I ____ly want to ______ it.

212 EBS 매일 10분 영어

unit 69. 영화 흥행

그 영화는 조기 종영 되었어.

The ________ was be taken ______ _____ly from

the theaters.

unit 70. 영화 배우

너 가장 좋아하는 영화 배우가 누구니?

________ is your ____vorite ____vie star?

unit 71. 음악 취향

나는 힙합 음악을 정말 좋아해요.

I am ______ly into ______-hop music.

unit 72. 좋아하는 가수

그 사람은 정말 대단한 가수인 거 같아.

I ________ he is an in______dible singer.

unit 73. 음악을 듣는 습관

나는 이제 음악을 어디서든 들을 수 있다.

I can ______ ____sten to ___sic wher______ I am.

unit 74. 음악 기기

선이 꼬이지 않아서 좋다.

I ______ it because the ______ do ______ get

______gled ____.

unit 75. K-POP

그들의 신곡은 여러 음악 차트 1위를 기록했다.

Their ______ song ____ No.1 on the ____sic charts.

이현석의 정면돌파 스피킹 213

테마별 짧은 영작에서 익힌 문장의
강세를 생각하며 빈칸을 콕콕 채워 봅니다.

이현석의 정면돌파스피킹을 만나는 방법

- EBS TV 시청
  EBS2TV
  EBS english
- 모바일/PC VOD 이용
  www.ebse.co.kr
- 오픈 단체 카톡방
  - 이현석선생님과 실시간 채팅

VOD 무료, MP3 다운로드 활용법

Step 1

EBSe.co.kr 또는 EBSe앱을 다운받아 접속 후, 로그인을 한다.

EBS 통합 아이디로 로그인 가능합니다.
아직 EBS 통합 아이디가 없으신 분은
회원가입 후 EBSe 모든 콘텐츠를
무료로 이용하실 수 있습니다.

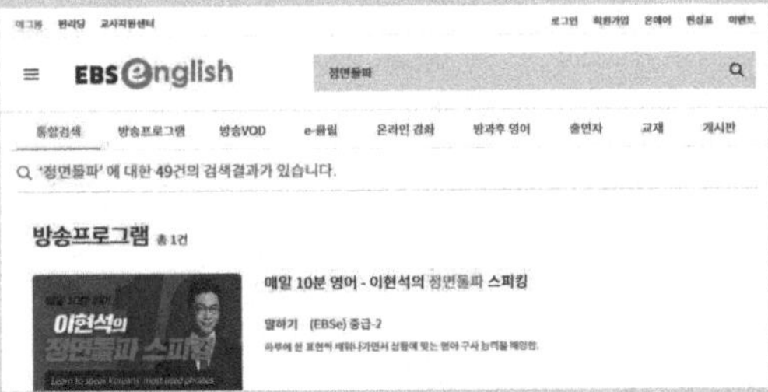

Step 2

<이현석의 정면돌파 스피킹>을 검색 후, 프로그램 페이지로 들어간다.

#이현석 #정면돌파
#정면돌파 스피킹

Step 3

<이현석의 정면돌파 스피킹> '다시보기'와 '다운로드' 메뉴를 마음껏! 무료로! 활용한다.

해당강의 : 발음강세 UNIT 66-150

※ **다시보기** : PC, 스마트폰으로 언제, 어디서든 강의 영상 시청이 가능합니다.

※ **다운로드** : 강의 음성 파일(mp3)을 미리 전자기기에 담아 인터넷 접속 환경이 아닌 곳에서도 학습할 수 있습니다.

여가 생활편

Movies
영화

unit 66 ~ unit 70

unit 66. 영화 장르

unit 67. 영화관

unit 68. 영화 감상

unit 69. 영화 흥행

unit 70. 영화 배우

66

영화 장르

STEP 1 주제어 핵심 단어 학습 발음 / 강세 훈련

영화	movie / film
속편	sequel
액션 영화	action movie
공포 영화	horror film
공상과학 영화	sci-fi movie
판타지 영화	fantasy movie
수퍼히어로 영화	superhero movie
애니메이션	animation
로맨틱 코미디	romantic comedy
대작	blockbuster
영화광	movie buff

STEP 2 짧은 영작 연습 발음 / 강세 훈련

(1) 나는 공포 영화는 별로 안 좋아해.
(sci-fi movie)
I am not a big fan of horror movies.

(2) 나는 로맨틱 코미디 영화를 즐겨 봐.
(romantic comedy)
I enjoy watching romantic comedies.

(3) 나는 영화를 정말 좋아하는 영화광이다.
(movie buff)
I am a huge movie buff.

STEP 3 짧은 대화 연습 발음 / 강세 훈련

A Do you want to catch a movie?
B Sure, why not? I'm a huge **movie buff**.
A Oh, really?
What types of movies do you like to watch?
B I watch almost all genres,
but I am not a big fan of **sci-fi movies**.

A 영화나 한편 볼까?
B 그러자. 못 볼 거 없지. 나 영화 엄청 좋아해.
A 아, 정말? 어떤 영화 장르 좋아하는데?
B 거의 모든 장르 다 보는데, 공상과학 영화는 별로 안 좋아해.

67

영화관

STEP 1 주제어 핵심 단어 학습 발음 / 강세 훈련

영화관	movie theater / cinema
영화표	movie ticket
영화 앱	movie app
티켓 카운터	ticket booth
다음 상영시간	next showing
마지막 상영시간	last showing
심야 상영시간	late-night showing
앞좌석 / 뒷좌석	front seats / back seats

STEP 2 짧은 영작 연습 발음 / 강세 훈련

(1) 한국에는 3대 영화관 체인망이 있다.
(movie theater)
There are three movie theater chains in Korea.

(2) 매표소 옆에 간식 파는 곳이 아마 있을 거야.
(ticket booth)
There should be a snack bar
next to the ticket booth.

(3) 그 영화 다음 상영시간이 몇 시니?
(next showing)
When is the next showing for that movie?

STEP 3 짧은 대화 연습 발음 / 강세 훈련

A I got the **movie tickets** on the app.
B Good. What time does it start?
A It starts at 6 o'clock. Is the time okay?
B Oh, that's too early. I get off at 5:30.
When is the **next showing**?

A 앱으로 영화표 샀어.
B 응. 영화 몇 시에 시작이니?
A 6시에 시작이야. 시간 괜찮아?
B 너무 이른 거 같아. 나 5시 30분에 퇴근해.
그 다음 상영시간이 몇 시니?

68 영화 감상

STEP 1 주제어 핵심 단어 학습 발음 / 강세 훈련

예고편	preview / trailer
개봉일 첫 상영 / 시사회	premier
줄거리	storyline
대반전	big twist
대박 영화	killer movie
흥미진진한	entertaining
감동적인	touching
눈물을 멈출 수 없었다	could not stop my tears
크게 웃었다	crack up

STEP 2 짧은 영작 연습 발음 / 강세 훈련

(1) 그 영화 예고편 봤는데, 정말 보고 싶어

(trailer)

I watched the trailer for that movie, and I really want to see it.

(2) 막판에 큰 반전이 있어서 줄거리가 마음에 들었어.

(storyline / big twist)

I liked the storyline because there was a big twist at the end.

(3) 영화가 감동적이어서 눈물을 참을 수 없었어.

(touching / could not stop my tears)

The movie was very touching, so I could not stop my tears.

STEP 3 짧은 대화 연습 발음 / 강세 훈련

A So, how was the movie? Did you like it?

B You bet. I think it was a **killer movie!**

A I think so too. I really liked the **big twist.**

B It was a little sad and **touching** at the end though. **I could not stop my tears.**

A 영화 재미 괜찮았어? 재미 있었니?

B 응! 정말 대박 영화였던 거 같아.

A 나도 그렇게 생각해. 대반전이 인상적이었어.

B 그런데 마지막에는 조금 슬프고 감동적이었어. 눈물을 참을 수가 없었어.

69

영화 흥행

STEP 1 주제어 핵심 단어 학습 발음 / 강세 훈련

개봉하다	be released
개봉일	release date
개봉 주	opening week
흥행에 성공하다	do very well at the box office
흥행작	box-office hit
표 판매 기록을 갈아 치우다	break ticket sales records
매진 되다	be sold-out
흥행에 실패하다	do terrible at the box office
조기 종영되다	be taken down early

STEP 2 짧은 영작 연습 발음 / 강세 훈련

(1) 속편 언제 개봉하는지 아니?

(be released)

Do you know when the sequel will be released?

(2) 그 영화는 흥행에 크게 성공했다.

(do very well at the box office)

The movie did very well at the box office.

(3) 그 영화는 조기 종영 되었어.

(be taken down early)

The movie was be taken down early from the theaters.

STEP 3 짧은 대화 연습 발음 / 강세 훈련

A Do you know when the **sequel** will **be released**?

B I heard it's going to **be released next** month.

A Really? I can't wait to watch it.

B Yeah, the first movie **did very well at the box office.** It was a huge **box-office hit.**

A 속편이 언제 개봉하는지 알아?

B 다음 달에 개봉한다고 들었어.

A 정말? 빨리 보고 싶다.

B 응. 첫번 작품이 정말 크게 성공했잖아.
대흥행작이었지.

70

영화 배우

STEP 1 주제어 핵심 단어 학습 발음 / 강세 훈련

영화 배우	movie star / actor / actress
주연 배우	leading actor
조연 배우	supporting actor
감독	director
배역	role
출연진	cast
연기력	acting
카메오 출연	cameo appearance
아카데미 시상식	the Academy Awards / the Oscars

STEP 2 짧은 영작 연습 발음 / 강세 훈련

(1) 너 가장 좋아하는 영화 배우가 누구니?
(movie star)
Who is your favorite movie star?

(2) 그가 그 영화의 남자 주인공으로 선정되었어.
(leading actor)
He was chosen as the leading actor of the movie.

(3) 출연진 전체의 연기력이 정말 마음에 들었어.
(acting / cast)
I really liked the acting of the entire cast.

STEP 3 짧은 대화 연습 발음 / 강세 훈련

A I think *Bohemian Rhapsody* was an incredible movie.
B Yeah, the **acting** by *Rami Malek* was amazing.
A **Didn't** he **win** an award for his **role** in the **film**?
B **Yes**, he **did**. He **won** **the Academy Award** for **Best Actor**.

A 보헤미안 랩소디 영화 정말 멋진 영화였던 거 같아.
B 응, 주연배우 라미 말렉의 연기가 정말 대단했지.
B 그 영화 배역으로 상 받지 않았나?
A 상 받았지. 아카데미 시상식에서 남우주연상 받았어.

매일 10분 영어 이현석의

정면돌파 스피킹

www.ebse.co.kr

여가 생활편

Music
음악

unit 71 ~ unit 75

71

음악 취향

STEP 1 주제어 핵심 단어 학습 발음 / 강세 훈련

팝 음악	pop music
힙합 음악	hip-hop music
락 음악	rock music
고전 음악	classical music
음악 취향	taste in music
멜로디	melody
가사	lyrics
신나는 곡	upbeat song
잔잔한 곡	slow song

STEP 2 짧은 영작 연습 발음 / 강세 훈련

(1) 나는 힙합 음악을 정말 좋아해요.
(hip-hop music)
I am really into hip-hop music.

(2) 그 노래 멜로디하고 가사가 너무 좋아.
(melody / lyrics)
I really like the melody and the lyrics of that song.

(3) 신나는 곡 좋아하세요, 잔잔한 곡 좋아하세요?
(upbeat song / slow song)
Do you like upbeat songs or slow songs?

STEP 3 짧은 대화 연습 발음 / 강세 훈련

A What kind of music do you like?
B I am really into **hip-hop music.**
A Is that what you are listening to right now?
B Yeah, this is my favorite song.
I really like the **melody**
and the **lyrics** of this song.

A 음악 뭐 좋아해?
B 나 힙합 음악 정말 좋아해.
A 지금 듣고 있는 것도 그거인가?
B 응. 내가 가장 좋아하는 곡이야.
이 곡 멜로디하고 가사가 너무 좋아.

72 좋아하는 가수

STEP 1 주제어 핵심 단어 학습 발음 / 강세 훈련

가수	singer / musician / artist / band
아이돌 그룹	boy group / girl group
열성팬이다	be a huge fan of
대단한 가수	incredible singer
대단한 댄서	amazing dancer
관중을 열광케 하다	make the crowd go crazy
가장 잘 알려진	one of the most well-known
개성 있는 목소리	unique voice
신곡(앨범)을 발표하다	release a new single (album)

STEP 2 짧은 영작 연습 발음 / 강세 훈련

(1) 그 사람은 정말 대단한 가수인 거 같아.
(incredible singer)
I think he is an incredible singer.

(2) 그들은 라이브 공연을 해서 관중을 열광하게 만들어.
(make the crowd go crazy)
They make the crowd go crazy at live concerts.

(3) 그녀는 최근에 신곡을 발표했다.
(release a new single)
She released a new single recently.

STEP 3 짧은 대화 연습 발음 / 강세 훈련

A Who's your favorite singer?
B I'm a huge fan of a Korean singer called Park Hyo Shin.
A Oh, really?
B Yes! He is an **amazing singer.** He **makes the crowd go crazy** at live concerts.

A 가장 좋아하는 가수가 누구니?
B 나 박효신이라는 한국가수의 큰 팬이야.
A 아 정말?
B 응. 정말 대단한 가수야.
라이브 공연에서 관중을 정말 열광하게 만들어.

73 음악을 듣는 습관

STEP 1 주제어 핵심 단어 학습 발음 / 강세 훈련

음악을 듣다	listen to music
음악을 틀어 놓는다	have some music on
어디 있든 간에	wherever I am
원할 때 언제든지	whenever I want to
이동 중에	when I'm on the move
버스나 지하철에서	when I'm on the subway or the bus
운전할 때 차 안에서	in the car when I'm driving
작업을 하거나 공부할 때	when I study or work
샤워를 할 때	when I'm taking a shower

STEP 2 짧은 영작 연습 발음 / 강세 훈련

(1) 나는 음악을 언제든지 들을 수 있다.
(whenever I want to)
I can listen to music whenever I want to.

(2) 나는 이제 음악을 어디서든 들을 수 있다.
(wherever I am)
I can now listen to music wherever I am.

(3) 이동 중에 음악을 주로 듣는 편입니다.
(when I'm on the move)
I usually listen to music when I'm on the move.

STEP 3 짧은 대화 연습 발음 / 강세 훈련

A When do you normally listen to music?
B Oh, I do that when I'm on the move.
A I see. Do you listen to music when you drive?
B Yes, I like to have some music on in the car when I'm driving.

A 음악을 주로 언제 듣니?
B 주로 이동할 때 들어.
A 그렇구나. 운전할 때 음악 듣니?
B 응. 운전할 때 차안에서 음악을 틀어 놔.

74 음악 기기

STEP 1 주제어 핵심 단어 학습 발음 / 강세 훈련

휴대용 기기	cell phones / laptops / tablet PCs
디지털 음악	digital music
스트리밍 사이트	streaming site
무선 이어폰	wireless earphones
무선 스피커	wireless speakers
블루투스 기능	Bluetooth function
꼽다	plug in
꼬이지 않는다	do not get tangled up
배터리가 닳다	run out of battery
정기적으로 충전하다	charge regularly

STEP 2 짧은 영작 연습 발음 / 강세 훈련

(1) 많은 사람들이 요즘 무선 이어폰이나 스피커를 쓴다.
(wireless earphones / wireless speakers)
Many people use wireless earphones or wireless speakers these days.

(2) 선이 꼬이지 않아서 좋다.
(do not get tangled up)
I like it because the wires do not get tangled up.

(3) 배터리가 달아서, 정기적으로 충전을 해야 한다.
(run out of battery / charge regularly)
They run out of battery, so I have to charge them regularly.

STEP 3 짧은 대화 연습 발음 / 강세 훈련

A Are those **wireless earphones**?

B Yeah, they are really convenient.
I don't have to **plug** them **in**.

A I know. The wires do **not get tangled up**, right?

B Exactly. I have to **charge** them **regularly** though.

A 그거 무선 이어폰이니?
B 응. 정말 편리해. 꼽을 필요가 없어.
A 알아. 선이 꼬일 일이 없지, 그렇지?
B 맞아. 물론 정기적으로 충전을 하긴 해야 해.

75

K-POP

STEP 1 주제어 핵심 단어 학습 발음 / 강세 훈련

한류 열풍	Korean pop-culture wave
해외에서 인기이다	be popular overseas
큰 인기를 끌고 있는	immensely popular
엄청난 인기를 누리다	create a sensation
선풍적 인기를 누리는	sensational
전 세계 각지에 팬이 있다	have fans all across the world
음악 차트 1위를 하다	hit No.1 on the music charts
음반 판매가 가장 많은 가수	best-selling artist

STEP 2 짧은 영작 연습 발음 / 강세 훈련

(1) 한국 음악은 전 세계적으로 선풍적인 인기를 누리고 있다.
(create a sensation / all across the world)
K-POP is creating a sensation all across the world.

(2) 한국 가수들은 해외에서 큰 인기를 누리고 있다.
(immensely popular)
Korean singers are immensely popular overseas.

(3) 그들의 신곡은 여러 음악 차트 1위를 기록했다.
(hit No.1 on the music charts)
Their new song hit No.1 on the music charts.

STEP 3 짧은 대화 연습 발음 / 강세 훈련

A K-POP is **creating a sensation** overseas.

B I know. Korean singers have fans **all across the world.**

A Yeah, their songs are **hitting No.1 on the music charts.**

B That's right. Some become **immensely popular.**

A K-POP은 해외에서 큰 돌풍을 일으키고 있어.
B 알아. 한국 가수들은 전 세계에 팬들을 확보하고 있어.
A 그들의 곡은 여러 음악 차트에서 1위를 계속 하고 있어.
B 맞아. 일부 곡들은 정말 엄청난 인기를 누리더라고.

매일 10분 영어 이현석의

정면돌파 스피킹

www.ebse.co.kr

여가 생활편

TV
방송

unit 76 ~ unit 80

unit 76. 방송 취향

unit 77. 방송 시청

unit 78. 뉴스 방송

unit 79. 방송 변화

unit 80. 인터넷 방송

76 방송 취향

STEP 1 주제어 핵심 단어 학습 발음 / 강세 훈련

방송하다	be on (TV)
뉴스 방송	news program
예능 방송	comedy program
토크쇼	talk show
요리 방송	cooking show
음악 방송	music show
스포츠 방송	sports show
오디션 방송	star audition program
만화영화	cartoon
드라마	drama
시청자	viewer

STEP 2 짧은 영작 연습 발음 / 강세 훈련

(1) 내가 가장 좋아하는 방송 오늘 방송해.
(be on)
My favorite show is on tonight.

(2) 나는 요리 방송과 오디션 방송을 즐겨 본다.
(cooking show / star audition program)
I like watching cooking shows and star audition programs.

(3) 우리 아이들은 만화 영화를 매일 본다.
(cartoons)
My children watch cartoons every day.

STEP 3 짧은 대화 연습 발음 / 강세 훈련

A What kinds of TV programs do you normally watch?
B Oh, I like to watch shows that make me laugh.
A You mean **comedy programs** or **talk shows**?
B Yes, I watch those types of shows most often.

A 무슨 TV 방송 주로 보니?
B 난 웃게 만들어 주는 방송 주로 봐.
A 예능 방송이나 토크쇼 같은 거?
B 응. 그런 방송 가장 자주 봐.

77

방송 시청

STEP 1 주제어 핵심 단어 학습 발음 / 강세 훈련

TV를 보다	watch TV
TV를 틀어 놓다	have the TV on
채널을 맞추다	tune in to
놓치다	miss
재방송	re-run
다시보기	VOD service
방송편	episode
리모컨	remote control
채널을 넘겨가며 보다	flip through channels

STEP 2 짧은 영작 연습 발음 / 강세 훈련

(1) 나는 저녁 먹을 때 TV 틀어 놓는 것을 좋아해.
(have the TV on)
I like to have the TV on when I'm having dinner.

(2) 지난번 방송을 놓쳐서, 다시보기로 볼 거야.
(miss / episode)
I missed the last episode, so I'm going to watch it through the VOD service.

(3) 그냥 채널을 넘겨가며 보고 있어.
(flip through channels)
I am just flipping through channels.

STEP 3 짧은 대화 연습 발음 / 강세 훈련

A Did you watch the final episode last night?
B No, I missed it. I fell asleep early. Was it fun?
A Oh, you bet! You should watch it!
B I will. I'll use the VOD service on my phone.

A 어젯밤에 마지막 회 봤니?
B 아니, 놓쳤어. 일찍 잠들어 버렸어. 재미 있었니?
A 응, 정말 재미 있었어. 꼭 봐!
B 그래야 겠다. 휴대전화로 다시보기 해서 봐야 겠다.

78

뉴스 방송

STEP 1 주제어 핵심 단어 학습 발음 / 강세 훈련

뉴스를 시청하다	watch the news
경제 뉴스	business news
스포츠 뉴스	sports news
연예 뉴스	entertainment news
일기예보	weather forecast
현안에 뒤처지지 않다	keep up with current affairs
식견을 넓혀주다	give me more insight
실시간으로 뉴스를 접하다	get the news (in) real time
정보를 얻게 되는	informative
도움이 되는	helpful

STEP 2 짧은 영작 연습 발음 / 강세 훈련

(1) 뉴스 방송은 현안에 뒤쳐지지 않게 해 준다.
(keep up with current affairs)
News programs help me keep up with current affairs.

(2) 이제는 뉴스를 실시간으로 접할 수 있다.
(get the news (in) real time)
We can get the news (in) real time now.

(3) 그 뉴스 보도는 정말 많은 것을 알게 해줬어.
(informative)
That news report was very informative.

STEP 3 짧은 대화 연습 발음 / 강세 훈련

A Do you watch the news regularly?
B Oh, yes! I try to **keep up with current affairs.**
A Do you check the news on your phone?
B Yes, I normally do that.
I can **get the news in real time** that way.

A 뉴스 주기적으로 보니?
B 그럼! 현안에 뒤쳐지지 않으려고 해.
A 휴대전화로 뉴스 확인하니?
B 응. 주로 그렇게 해. 그러면 실시간으로 뉴스를 접할 수 있으니까.

79

방송 변화

STEP 1 주제어 핵심 단어 학습 발음 / 강세 훈련

구식인	old-fashioned
몇 안 되는 채널	very few channels
케이블/위성 방송	cable TV / satellite TV
수백 개의 채널	hundreds of channels
재미있고 흥미진진한	fun and entertaining
다양한 선택의 폭	a lot of options
온갖 종류의 방송	all sorts of shows
몰라보게 발전해 왔다	have come a long way

STEP 2 짧은 영작 연습 발음 / 강세 훈련

(1) 정말 재미있고 흥미진진한 방송이 많아.

(fun and entertaining)

There are so many shows that are fun and entertaining.

(2) 이제는 하루 언제든지 온갖 종류의 방송을 즐겨볼 수 있다.

(all sorts of shows)

We can now enjoy all sorts of shows 24/7.

(3) TV 방송은 정말 몰라보게 발전해 왔다.

(have come a long way)

TV programs have come a long way.

STEP 3 짧은 대화 연습 발음 / 강세 훈련

A TV shows are so **fun and entertaining** these days.

B I agree. They **have come a long way.**

A We now have cable and satellite TV, so there are so many channels.

B Right. We can now enjoy **all sorts of shows** 24/7.

A TV 방송이 요즘 정말 재미있고 흥미진진해.
B 맞아. 정말 몰라보게 발전해 왔어.
A 이제는 케이블TV와 위성TV가 있어서, 채널이 정말 많아.
B 그렇지. 이제 하루 언제든 온갖 종류의 방송을 즐겨볼 수 있잖아.

80

인터넷 방송

STEP 1 주제어 핵심 단어 학습 발음 / 강세 훈련

인터넷	TV Internet TV
유튜브 / 유튜버	YouTube / YouTuber
채널에 구독하다	subscribe to a channel
업데이트를 받다	get regular updates
조회수	hits / views
넷플릭스	Netflix
정기구독하고 있다	have a subscription
미국 방송	American TV shows
~에 중독되다	be hooked on

STEP 2 짧은 영작 연습 발음 / 강세 훈련

(1) 나는 유튜브에서 구독하는 채널이 몇 개 있다.
(subscribe to a channel)
There are several channels I subscribe to on YouTube.

(2) 나는 넷플릭스를 정기구독하고 있어.
(have a subscription)
I have a subscription on Netflix.

(3) 나 미드에 중독이 된 거 같아.
(be hooked on / American TV shows)
I think I am hooked on American TV shows.

STEP 3 짧은 대화 연습 발음 / 강세 훈련

A Do you have a **YouTube channel** you **subscribe to**?

B No, I don't. Do you?

A Yeah, there are many fun channels you can watch.

B I **have a subscription** on **Netflix** though.

A 유튜브에서 구독하는 채널 있니?
B 아니 없어. 너는?
A 응. 볼 수 있는 재미 있는 채널이 많아.
B 나 넷플릭스 정기구독 중이기는 해.

매일 10분 영어 이현석의

정면돌파 스피킹

www.ebse.co.kr

여가 생활편

Sports

스포츠

unit 81 ~ unit 85

81

경기 관람

STEP 1 주제어 핵심 단어 학습 발음 / 강세 훈련

야구 경기장에 가다	go to a baseball game
축구 경기를 관람하다	watch a soccer match
국가대표팀을 응원하다	cheer for one's national team
단체로 응원하다	cheer in groups
거리에 모이다	gather in the streets
대규모 길거리 응원전	large-scale street cheering
열기가 달아 오르다	get heated up
막대풍선	stick balloon

STEP 2 짧은 영작 연습 발음 / 강세 훈련

(1) 주말에 야구 보러 갔어.

(go to a baseball game)

I went to a baseball game over the weekend.

(2) 우리나라 팀을 길거리 응원하러 갔다.

(gather in the streets)

We gathered in the streets
to cheer for national team.

(3) 분위기가 달아 올랐다.

(get heated up)

The mood got heated up.

STEP 3 짧은 대화 연습 발음 / 강세 훈련

A Are you going to watch the big soccer match tonight?

B Of course! My friends and I are going to **gather in the streets.**

A Great! Maybe I will join you.

B You should.
Cheering for our national team is so fun.

A 오늘 저녁에 축구 경기 볼 거니?
B 물론이지! 친구들하고 길거리 응원하러 갈 거야.
A 멋지네. 나도 같이 가야 겠다.
B 그래. 국가대표팀 경기를 응원하는 것은 정말 재미있어.

82

야구

STEP 1 주제어 핵심 단어 학습 발음 / 강세 훈련

야구	baseball
타자 / 주자	hitter / runner
투수 / 포수	pitcher / catcher
2회초	in the top of 2nd inning
3회말	in the bottom of the 3rd inning
득점하다	score a run
1루타 / 2루타 / 3루타	single / double / triple
3점 홈런	3-run homerun
만루홈런	grand slam
타점	RBI (runner batted in)
방어율	ERA (earned run average)

STEP 2 짧은 영작 연습 발음 / 강세 훈련

(1) 우리 팀이 5회초에 2득점을 했다.

(in the top of 5th inning)

Our team scored two runs in the top of 5th inning.

(2) 그는 오늘 1타점 2루타를 쳤다.

(RBI double)

He hit an RBI double today.

(3) 그는 현재 메이저리그에서 방어율이 가장 낮다.

(ERA)

He currently has the lowest ERA in the Major League.

STEP 3 짧은 대화 연습 발음 / 강세 훈련

A Did you see Ryu Hyun-jin throw this morning?

B Yes, he did great! He **pitched 8 innings** without allowing any runs.

A I know! He **stuck out 9 hitters.**

B I think he's amazing this season. He currently has the lowest **ERA** in the Major League.

A 오늘 아침에 류현진 던지는 거 봤니?

B 응. 정말 잘했어. 8이닝 무실점 경기였잖아.

A 알아! 탈삼진도 8개나 기록했고.

B 올 시즌 정말 놀라울 정도로 잘하는 거 같아. 메이저리그 통틀어서 방어율이 가장 낮잖아.

83 축구

STEP 1 주제어 핵심 단어 학습 발음 / 강세 훈련

축구	football / soccer
전반전에	in the first half
후반전에	in the second half
득점하다	score a goal
실점하다	give up a goal
경기를 앞서가다	lead the game
동점을 만들다	tie the game
경기를 역전시키다	turn the game around
2대 0으로 이기다	win the game 2 to 0
3대 1로 지다	lose the game 3 to 1

STEP 2 짧은 영작 연습 발음 / 강세 훈련

(1) 우리는 전반에 2골을 넣었다.

(score a goal)

We scored two goals in the first half.

(2) 후반전에 동점골을 넣었다.

(tie the game)

We tie the game in the second half.

(3) 우리 팀이 꼭 역전시켰으면 좋겠다.

(turn the game around)

I really hope our team turns the game around.

STEP 3 짧은 대화 연습 발음 / 강세 훈련

A We **gave up a goal** in **the first half**, right?

B Yeah, but we tied the game in **the second half**.

A So, what was the final score?

B We did really well, but we **lost 2 to 1**.

A 우리가 전반전에 한 골 먹었지?

B 응. 그런데 후반전에 동점골을 넣었어.

A 그래서 최종 스코어가 어떻게 됐어?

B 정말 잘하기는 했는데, 2대 1로 졌어.

84 농구

STEP 1 주제어 핵심 단어 학습 발음 / 강세 훈련

농구	basketball
쿼터	quarter
공격 / 수비	offense / defense
30득점하다	score 30 points
3점 슛	three pointer
자유투	free throw
버저 비터	buzzer beater
턴오버	turnover
트리플더블	triple double
공이 밖으로 나가다	go out of bounds
파울을 하다	commit a foul
심판	referee

STEP 2 짧은 영작 연습 발음 / 강세 훈련

(1) 그는 3쿼터에만 12점을 넣었어.

(quarter / score points)

He scored 12 points in the third quarter alone.

(2) 공이 밖으로 나갔다.

(go out of bounds)

The ball went out of bounds.

(3) 그는 4번째 파울을 범했어.

(commit a foul)

He committed his fourth foul.

STEP 3 짧은 대화 연습 발음 / 강세 훈련

A Did you see the basketball match yesterday?

B Yes! Our favorite player did really well.

A That's right. He scored 33 points.
He got five three-pointers as well.

B He nearly did a triple double.

A 어제 농구 결승전 봤니?

B 응! 우리가 가장 좋아하는 선수가 너무 잘했어.

A 맞아. 33득점이나 했잖아. 3점 슛도 5개나 성공시키고.

B 트리플 더블도 할 뻔 했잖아.

85

테니스

STEP 1 주제어 핵심 단어 학습 발음 / 강세 훈련

단식 경기	singles
복식 경기	doubles
8강	quarter-finals
4강	semi-finals
결승	final match
서브 에이스	serve ace
득점 샷	winner
실책	unforced error
심판	umpire
타이브레이크	tie break

STEP 2 짧은 영작 연습 발음 / 강세 훈련

(1) 나는 단식보다는 복식 경기를 더 자주 해.
(singles / doubles)
I play doubles instead of singles more often.

(2) 그 선수는 오늘 실책이 조금 많았어.
(unforced error)
The player had a lot of unforced errors today.

(3) 그는 메이저 대회 준결승에 진출했다.
(semi-finals)
He reached the semi-finals at a major tournament.

STEP 3 짧은 대화 연습 발음 / 강세 훈련

A I watched the US OPEN men's final match last night.
B Yeah, I saw it too. It was a full-set match.
A That's right.
They went into the tie break in the fifth set.
B Uh-huh. It was one of the best matches I have seen in my life.

A 어제 US오픈 남자 결승전 경기 봤어.
B 응. 나도 봤어. 플 세트 접전을 펼쳤잖아.
A 맞아. 5세트에 타이브레이크까지 갔지.
B 맞아. 내가 지금까지 본 경기 중에 최고의 경기였어.

매일 10분 영어 이현석의

정면돌파 스피킹

www.ebse.co.kr

여가 생활편

Social Media
소셜 미디어

unit 86 ~ unit 90

86

소셜 미디어 활동

STEP 1 주제어 핵심 단어 학습 발음 / 강세 훈련

소셜 미디어	social media
소셜 네트워크	social networking service (SNS)
계정	account
게시물	posting
게시하다	post up
공유하다	repost / share
원본 게시물	original post
댓글을 달다	leave a comment
좋아요를 누르다	press the 'like' button
엄청나게 확산되다	go viral

STEP 2 짧은 영작 연습 발음 / 강세 훈련

(1) 나는 소셜 미디어 게시물을 자주 올리는 편이야.
(social media / post up)
I post up things on social media quite often.

(2) 나는 그 게시물을 내 페이지에 공유했어.
(repost)
I reposted that posting on my page.

(3) 댓글을 남기거나 좋아요를 자주 누르는 편이야.
(leave a comment / press the 'like' button)
I leave a comment or press the 'like' button quite often.

STEP 3 짧은 대화 연습 발음 / 강세 훈련

A Your **posting** was so funny! I **reposted** it!
B Oh, did you? I'm glad you liked it.
A So many people **pressed the 'like'** button.
B Yeah, I didn't know that so many people would like it.

A 네가 올린 게시물 너무 웃겼어. 그거 공유했어.
B 아 그래? 마음에 들었다니 다행이네.
A 정말 많은 사람들이 '좋아요'를 눌렀어.
B 응, 그렇게 많은 사람들이 좋아할지는 몰랐어.

87

페이스북

STEP 1 주제어 핵심 단어 학습 발음 / 강세 훈련

페이스북을 하다	be on Facebook
프로필	profile
친구를 맺다	friend someone
친구를 끊다	unfriend someone
팔로우 하다	follow someone
상태 업데이트	status update
타임 라인	timeline
뉴스 피드	news feed
개인 메시지를 보내다	send a private message (PM)

STEP 2 짧은 영작 연습 발음 / 강세 훈련

(1) 너 페이스북 하니?

(be on Facebook)

Are you on Facebook?

(2) 그 친구가 나를 친구 취소한 것을 알았어.

(unfriend someone)

I found out that he unfriended me.

(3) 타임 라인에 뉴스 피드가 올라와.

(timeline / news feed)

There is news feed on the timeline.

STEP 3 짧은 대화 연습 발음 / 강세 훈련

A Did you friend me on Facebook?

B Yes. I checked your profile and added you as a friend.

A I'll do that too.

B I also sent you a PM.

A 나 친구 페북 추가했어?

B 응. 프로필 확인하고 추가했어.

A 나도 할게.

B 개인메세지로 하나 보냈어.

88 인스타그램

STEP 1 주제어 핵심 단어 학습 발음 / 강세 훈련

인스타	Instagram (IG)
팔로우 하다 / 팔로어	follow / follower
사용자명	username (handle)
게시물	post
태그하다	tag @
해시태그	hashtag #
더블탭	double tap
이모티콘	emoji
갤러리	gallery
스토리	story
하이라이트	highlight

STEP 2 짧은 영작 연습 발음 / 강세 훈련

(1) 인스타 팔로어가 몇 명이니?
(follower)
How many followers do you have on Instagram?

(2) 그 게시물에 너 태그 했어.
(tag)
I tagged you on the posting.

(3) 나는 게시물에 해시태그 여러 개 하는 편이야.
(hashtag)
I hashtag a lot of words on my posts.

STEP 3 짧은 대화 연습 발음 / 강세 훈련

A I saw your **posting** on Instagram.
B Yeah, I **tagged you** on the **posting**.
A I **double tapped** it as soon as I saw it.
B Yeah, I saw your **comment** with the pretty **emojis**.

A 인스타에 너의 게시물 봤어.
B 응. 그 게시물에 너 태그했어.
A 보자마자 좋아요 눌렀지!
B 응. 예쁜 이모티콘 쓴 댓글 봤어.

89 트위터

STEP 1 주제어 핵심 단어 학습 발음 / 강세 훈련

트위터 메시지	tweet
리트윗하다	retweet (RT)
팔로우 / 언팔하다	follow / unfollow
팔로어	follower
피드	feed
답글을 달다	reply
개인 메시지	direct message
유행처럼 퍼지다	trend / trending
내 생각에는	IMO (in my opinion)
솔직히	TBH (to be honest)

STEP 2 짧은 영작 연습 발음 / 강세 훈련

(1) 네 트윗 여러 번 리트윗 되고 있어.

(retweet)

Your tweet is being retweeted many times.

(2) 그 문구가 지금 퍼지고 있어.

(trending)

That phrase is trending right now.

(3) 그 사람 팔로우 취소해야 할 거 같아.

(unfollow)

I think I should unfollow him.

STEP 3 짧은 대화 연습 발음 / 강세 훈련

A The phrase he tweeted is trending right now.

B Yeah, but he **tweets** at lot of messages.

A I know. Too many sometimes.

B I think I'm going to **unfollow** him.

A 그 친구가 트윗한 문구가 지금 유행하고 있어.

B 응, 그런데 그 친구 트윗을 정말 많이 올려.

A 알아. 가끔 너무 많이 올리지.

B 나 그 친구 팔로우 취소 할 거야.

90

유튜브

STEP 1 주제어 핵심 단어 학습 발음 / 강세 훈련

유튜브 / 유튜버	YouTube / YouTuber
채널을 구독하다	subscribe to a channel
구독 취소하다	unsubscribe
구독자	subscriber
시청자	viewer
조회수	hits / views
영상을 편집하다	edit a video clip
자막을 넣다	put in the subtitles
광고	ad
저작권	copyright

STEP 2 짧은 영작 연습 발음 / 강세 훈련

(1) 유튜브에 구독하는 채널 있니?
(subscribe to a channel)
Do you subscribe to any channels on YouTube?

(2) 그 영상은 백만이 넘는 조회수를 기록했다.
(views)
The clip got more than a million views.

(3) 영상 편집하고 자막 넣는데 정말 시간이 오래 걸려.
(edit a video clip / put in the subtitles)
It takes so much time to edit a video clip and put in the subtitles.

STEP 3 짧은 대화 연습 발음 / 강세 훈련

A Do you subscribe to any channels on YouTube?
B Yes, there are several I subscribe to.
A What are they about?
B Some are English-related and some are movie-related.

A 유튜브에서 구독하는 채널 있니?
B 응. 구독 채널 몇 개 있어.
A 무슨 종류 채널이니?
B 일부는 영어 관련이고, 일부는 영화 관련이야.

매일 10분 영어 이현석의

정면돌파 스피킹

www.ebse.co.kr

여가 생활편

Games
게임

unit 91 ~ unit 95

91 모바일 게임

STEP 1 주제어 핵심 단어 학습 발음 / 강세 훈련

온라인/모바일 게임	online game / mobile game
MMO 게임	massive multiplayer online game
RPG 게임	role playing game
스포츠 게임	sports game
퍼즐 게임	puzzle game
시뮬레이션 게임	simulation game
전략 게임	strategy game
슈팅 게임	shooting game
어드벤처 게임	adventure game
격투 게임	combat game
오락실 게임	arcade game

STEP 2 짧은 영작 연습 발음 / 강세 훈련

(1) 요즘 가장 인기 있는 모바일 게임이 뭐니?
(mobile game)
What is the hottest mobile game these days?

(2) 나는 RPG 게임을 정말 좋아한다.
(role playing game)
I am really into role playing games.

(3) 슈팅 게임 잘하는 편이니?
(shooting game)
Are you any good at shooting games?

STEP 3 짧은 대화 연습 발음 / 강세 훈련

A What is the hottest mobile game these days?

A I don't know about the hottest,
but I play this puzzle game a lot.

A Oh, I think I've seen that game before.

A It's very simple, but it's quite addictive.
I can't stop playing.

A 요즘 가장 뜨고 있는 모바일 게임이 뭐니?
B 글쎄, 가장 뜨고 있는 게임은 모르겠는데, 난 이 퍼즐 게임 자주 해.
A 아, 그거 예전에 본 적 있는 거 같아.
B 정말 간단한 게임인데, 제법 중독성이 있어. 계속 하게 돼.

92

게임 설치

STEP 1 주제어 핵심 단어 학습 발음 / 강세 훈련

게임 앱	game app
게임 광고	game ad
설치하다	install
삭제하다	uninstall / delete
재설치하다	reinstall
업데이트 패치	update patch
인앱 구매	in-app purchase
게임 콘솔	game console

STEP 2 짧은 영작 연습 발음 / 강세 훈련

(1) 그 게임 휴대폰에 지금 설치했어.

(install)

I installed that game on my phone.

(2) 업데이트 패치 나와서 게임을 재설치했어.

(update patch / reinstall)

I reinstalled the game
because there was an update patch.

(3) 게임 도중 현질을 하는 사람들도 있다.

(in-app purchase)

There are people who make in-app purchases
while playing games.

STEP 3 짧은 대화 연습 발음 / 강세 훈련

A Do you still play that game?

B No, I quit. I deleted it a few weeks ago.

A Maybe you got bored.

B I did. I saw the update patch last week though.
Maybe I should reinstall it.

A 그 게임 아직도 하니?
B 아니, 그만뒀어. 몇 주 전에 삭제했어.
A 흥미를 잃었나 보네.
B 응, 맞아. 그런데 지난 주에 업데이트 패치 나온 거 봤어. 재설치할까 생각 중이야.

93

게임 중독

STEP 1 주제어 핵심 단어 학습 발음 / 강세 훈련

게임 중독	game addiction
중독되다	be addicted to
중독성이 있는	addictive
혈안이 되다	be obsessed with
너무 많은 시간을 보내다	spend too much time
사회적 문제	social problem
청소년	teenager / youngster
금단 현상	withdrawal
상담 치료	counselling

STEP 2 짧은 영작 연습 발음 / 강세 훈련

(1) 나 이 게임에 중독된 거 같아.
(be addicted to)
I think I am addicted to this game.

(2) 많은 십대들이 게임에 너무 많은 시간을 허비해.
(spend too much time)
Many teenagers spend too much time on games.

(3) 게임 중독은 사회적 문제이다.
(game addiction / social problem)
Game addiction is a social problem.

STEP 3 짧은 대화 연습 발음 / 강세 훈련

A Oh, I think I am addicted to this game.
B Yeah, I see you play a lot.
A I think I am spending too much time on this game.
B Yeah, you should play a little less. Game addiction is a problem, you know.

A 아, 나 이 게임 중독된 거 같아.
B 응, 자주 하는 거 보이더라.
A 이 게임에 너무 시간을 많이 허비하는 거 같아.
B 맞아. 조금 덜 할 필요가 있어. 게임 중독 나름 문제인 거 알지?

94

프로게이머

STEP 1 주제어 핵심 단어 학습 발음 / 강세 훈련

프로게이머	professional gamer
프로리그	professional league
놀라운 반사신경	amazing reflexes
엄청난 인기를 누리다	be wildly popular
폭넓은 팬층이 있다	have a large fan base
게임 대회	game tournament
게임 채널	game channel
게임 방송	game broadcast

STEP 2 짧은 영작 연습 발음 / 강세 훈련

(1) 프로게이머들은 엄청난 반사신경을 가지고 있다.
(professional gamer / amazing reflexes)
Professional gamers have amazing reflexes.

(2) 일부 프로게이머들은 폭넓은 팬층이 있다.
(have a large fan base)
Some professional gamers have a large fan base.

(3) 대규모 게임 대회들이 게임 채널에서 중계된다.
(game tournament / game channel)
Big game tournaments are aired on game channels.

STEP 3 짧은 대화 연습 발음 / 강세 훈련

A What are you watching?

B Oh, it's a **game tournament.**
My favorite player is playing.

A Is he a **professional gamer?**

B Yes, he is. He has **amazing reflexes.**
It's unbelievable.

A 뭐 보니?
B 아, 이거 게임 대회야. 내가 가장 좋아하는 선수가 출전했어.
A 프로게이머야?
B 응, 맞아. 반사신경이 정말 엄청나. 믿기 힘들 정도야.

95

보드 게임

STEP 1 주제어 핵심 단어 학습 발음 / 강세 훈련

보드 게임	boardgame
보드 게임 카페	boardgame cafe
단체로 게임을 하다	play games in groups
주사위를 던지다	throw the dice
말을 옮기다	move one's piece
카드를 뽑다	draw a card
차례대로 하다	take turns
차례를 넘기다	miss a turn

STEP 2 짧은 영작 연습 발음 / 강세 훈련

(1) 너 주사위 두 번 던져야 해.
(throw the dice)
You have to throw the dice twice.

(2) 말을 5칸 앞으로 이동시켜.
(move one's piece)
Move your piece five slots forward.

(3) 카드에 너 한 차례 건너뛰라고 나와 있어.
(miss a turn)
The card says you should miss a turn.

STEP 3 짧은 대화 연습 발음 / 강세 훈련

A Okay, whose **turn** is it?
B It's **mine**. Let me **throw the dice**.
A Aha! You should **draw a card**!
What does it **say**?
B Oh, **no**! It **says** I should **miss a turn**.

A 누구 차례니?
B 내 차례야. 주사위 던질게.
A 아하! 카드 뽑아. 카드에 뭐라고 써 있니?
B 아이고! 한 차례 건너뛰라고 되어 있어.

매일 10분 영어 이현석의

정면돌파 스피킹

www.ebse.co.kr

여가 생활편

Vacation
휴가

unit 96 ~ unit 100

unit 96. 휴가 신청

unit 97. 휴가 계획

unit 98. 휴가 비용

unit 99. 휴가 에피소드

unit 100. 집에서 보내는 휴가

96

휴가 신청

STEP 1 주제어 핵심 단어 학습 발음 / 강세 훈련

휴가를 가다	take a vacation
휴가를 떠나다	go on a vacation
휴가 중이다	be on vacation
일주일 휴가를 내다	take a week off
며칠 휴가를 내다	take a few days off
병가를 내다	take a sick day
휴직하다	take a leave of absence
출산 휴가를 내다	take a maternity leave
육아 휴직을 내다	take a childcare leave

STEP 2 짧은 영작 연습 발음 / 강세 훈련

(1) 나 며칠 휴가 낼 생각이야.

(take a few days off)

I'm thinking of taking a few days off.

(2) 그 친구 독감 걸려서 병가를 냈어.

(take a sick day)

He took a sick day
because he came down with the flu.

(3) 그녀는 3개월간 출산 휴가를 냈어.

(take a maternity leave)

She took a maternity leave for three months.

STEP 3 짧은 대화 연습 발음 / 강세 훈련

A I am **taking a year off.**

B Oh, really? Are you **taking a leave of absence?**

A Yeah, I am **taking a childcare leave.**

B Oh, I see. I guess you need to spend more time with your baby.

A 나 1년 정도 쉴까 해.
B 아 정말? 휴직하는 거야?
A 응. 육아 휴직 내려고.
B 아, 그렇구나. 아기하고 보낼 시간이 더 필요하구나.

97

휴가 계획

STEP 1 주제어 핵심 단어 학습 발음 / 강세 훈련

휴가를 계획하다	plan a vacation
휴가 계획을 세우다	make vacation plans
여행 계획을 세우다	make travel plans
예약을 하다	make a reservation
호텔을 예약하다	book a hotel
항공권을 구매하다	get a plane ticket
여행사	travel agency
패키지 여행 상품	package trip

STEP 2 짧은 영작 연습 발음 / 강세 훈련

(1) 여름 휴가 계획 다 세웠니?

(make vacation plans)

Have you **made** va**ca**tion plans for the **sum**mer?

(2) 호텔 예약하고 항공권 구매했어.

(book a hotel / get a plane ticket)

I **book**ed a ho**tel** and **got** a **plane** ticket.

(3) 여행사 통해서 여행 패키지 상품으로 갈 거야.

(travel agency / package trip)

I am **go**ing to **go** on a **pack**age trip
through a **tra**vel agency.

STEP 3 짧은 대화 연습 발음 / 강세 훈련

A **Have** you **made vacation plans** for the **sum**mer?

B No, **not** yet. I **think** I may **go** on a **package trip**.

A Through a **travel agency**?

B **Yes!** **That's** the **ea**siest way I **think**.

A 여름 휴가 계획 다 세웠니?
B 아니, 아직. 패키지 여행 갈까 생각 중이야.
A 여행사 통해서?
B 응! 그게 가장 쉬운 방법인 거 같아.

98

휴가 비용

STEP 1 주제어 핵심 단어 학습 발음 / 강세 훈련

예산을 잡다	set a budget
돈을 쓰다	spend money on
비용을 초과하다	overspend
성수기	peak season
더 높은 요율	higher rates
할인을 받다	get a discount
좋은 가격에 사다	get a good deal
바가지를 쓰다	get ripped off
바가지	rip-off

STEP 2 짧은 영작 연습 발음 / 강세 훈련

(1) 여행갈 때 쓸 예산 정했니?
(set a budget)
Have you set a budget for your trip?

(2) 여행 중에 돈을 너무 많이 쓰고 싶지는 않아
(overspend)
I don't want to overspend during the trip.

(3) 나 바가지 쓴 거 같아.
(get ripped off)
I think I got ripped off.

STEP 3 짧은 대화 연습 발음 / 강세 훈련

A How was your vacation?
B It was great, but I think I **spent** too much **money on** shopping.
A Didn't you **set a budget** for the trip?
B I did, but I think I **overspent** on clothes on shoes.

A 휴가 어땠니?
B 정말 좋았는데, 쇼핑에 돈을 너무 많이 쓴 거 같아.
A 여행 예산을 정해 놓은 게 아니었어?
B 세웠지. 그런데, 옷하고 신발 사는데 돈을 지나치게 쓴 거 같아.

99 휴가 에피소드

STEP 1 주제어 핵심 단어 학습 발음 / 강세 훈련

길을 잃다	get lost
분실하다	lose something
두고 오다	leave something behind
몸이 아프다	get sick
식중독에 걸리다	get food poisoning
다치다	get injured
지연되다	be delayed
취소되다	be cancelled

STEP 2 짧은 영작 연습 발음 / 강세 훈련

(1) 공항에서 몇 차례나 길을 잃었어.
(get lost)
I got lost several times at the airport.

(2) 여권을 호텔방에 두고 나왔어.
(leave something behind)
I left my passport behind in the hotel room.

(3) 항공편이 연착이 되어서 문제가 생겼어.
(be delayed)
I had a problem because I flight was delayed.

STEP 3 짧은 대화 연습 발음 / 강세 훈련

A Did you enjoy your trip?
B No, I got sick. I got food poisoning.
A Oh, I'm so sorry to hear that.
B Plus, my return flight was delayed
and I had to wait for a long time at the airport.

A 여행 재미있었어?
B 아니. 나 아팠어. 식중독 걸렸어.
A 아이고, 안타깝네.
B 그리고 돌아오는 비행기가 연착이 되어서, 공항에서 한참 기다렸어.

100 집에서 보내는 휴가

STEP 1 주제어 핵심 단어 학습 발음 / 강세 훈련

집에서 휴가를 보내다	take a vacation at home
편하게 쉬다	kick back and relax
휴식을 취하다	get some rest
뜻깊은 시간을 보내다	spend some quality time
되돌아보다	look back on
푹 쉰 상태가 되다	feel well-rested
밀린 잠을 자다	catch up on some sleep
밀린 집안일을 하다	catch up on some housework
친구들과 자리를 함께 하다	get together with friends

STEP 2 짧은 영작 연습 발음 / 강세 훈련

(1) 그냥 집에서 편하게 쉴까 생각 중이야.
(kick back and relax)
I am just going to kick back and relax at home.

(2) 집에서 밀린 잠이나 조금 자고 싶어.
(catch up on some sleep)
I just want to catch up on some sleep.

(3) 가족들과 뜻깊은 시간을 함께 보낼까 해.
(spend some quality time)
I am planning on spending some quality time with my family.

STEP 3 짧은 대화 연습 발음 / 강세 훈련

A How was your vacation?
Did you do anything special?

B No, I just **kicked back and relaxed** at home.

A That's good! You needed to **get some rest.**

B Right. I did **spend some quality time** with my kids though.

A 휴가 어땠니? 뭐 특별한 거 했어?
B 아니, 그냥 집에서 편하게 쉬었어.
A 좋네. 너 휴식이 조금 필요했잖아.
B 맞아. 그대신 아이들과 뜻깊은 시간을 보내긴 했어.

매일 10분 영어 이현석의

정면돌파 스피킹

www.ebse.co.kr

여가
생활편

Online Shopping
인터넷 쇼핑

unit 101 ~ unit 105

101

인터넷 쇼핑몰

STEP 1 주제어 핵심 단어 학습 **발음 / 강세 훈련**

인터넷 쇼핑몰	online shopping mall
인터넷 쇼핑하다	shop online
회원 가입하다	sign up
판매자	seller
구매자	buyer
제품 후기	product review
주문하다 / 주문	order
구매하다 / 구매품	purchase
한정 판매	limited offer

STEP 2 짧은 영작 연습 발음 / 강세 훈련

(1) 인터넷 쇼핑 얼마나 자주 하니?
(shop online)
How often do you shop online?

(2) 나는 인터넷에서 물건을 사기 전에 항상 제품 후기를 읽어 본다.
(product review)
I always read the product reviews before I buy something online.

(3) 한정판으로 판매였던 거 같아.
(limited offer)
I think it was a limited offer.

STEP 3 짧은 대화 연습 발음 / 강세 훈련

A How often do you shop online?
B Well, I do that whenever I need to.
A Do you read product reviews before buying stuff?
B Yes, I always try to do that before I purchase something.

A 인터넷 쇼핑 얼마나 자주 하니?
B 글쎄, 필요할 때마다 해.
A 뭐 사기 전에 제품 후기 읽어보니?
B 응. 무엇인가 구매하기 전에 항상 그렇게 하려고 하는 편이야.

102

인터넷 결제

STEP 1 주제어 핵심 단어 학습 발음 / 강세 훈련

~을 결제하다	pay for something
신용카드로 결제하다	pay with one's credit card
결제를 하다	make a payment
결제를 취소하다	cancel a payment
할부로 결제하다	pay in installments
영수증	receipt
할인을 받다	get a discount
10% 할인을 받다	get 10 percent off
포인트 적립하다	accumulate points

STEP 2 짧은 영작 연습 발음 / 강세 훈련

(1) 그거 어떻게 결제할 거니?
(pay for something)
How are you going to pay for it?

(2) 나는 할부 결제하는 것을 별로 안 좋아해.
(pay in installments)
I don't like paying in installments.

(3) 지금 사면 10% 할인을 받을 수 있어.
(get 10 percent off)
You can get 10 percent off if you buy it now.

STEP 3 짧은 대화 연습 발음 / 강세 훈련

A You can get 10 percent off if you buy it online.
B I know. I'm going to buy it now.
A How are you going to pay for it?
B I'm going to pay with my credit card.

A 인터넷에서 사면, 10% 할인을 받을 수 있어.
B 알아. 지금 살 거야.
A 결제는 어떻게 할 거야?
B 내 신용카드로 결제를 할 거야.

103 인터넷 교환/환불

STEP 1 주제어 핵심 단어 학습 발음 / 강세 훈련

반품하다	send something back
교환하다	get an exchange
환불하다	get a refund
돈을 돌려 받다	get one's money back
불만족스러운	unsatisfied / unhappy
잘 안 맞다	not fit well
제대로 작동을 안 하다	not work well
기대와 다른	not what I expected

STEP 2 짧은 영작 연습 발음 / 강세 훈련

(1) 이 셔츠 반품할 거야.

(send something back)

I'm going to send this shirt back.

(2) 교환할 거니, 아니면 환불할 거니?

(get an exchange / get a refund)

Are you going to get an exchange or get a refund?

(3) 이 시계 내가 기대했던 것과는 다르네.

(not what I expected)

This watch is not what I expected.

STEP 3 짧은 대화 연습 발음 / 강세 훈련

A Are those new shoes?

B Yes, I bought them last week, but I'm going to **send them back.**

A Why? Don't you like them?

B **No**, they **are not what I expected.** I'm going to **get a refund.**

A 그거 새 신발이니?

B 응. 지난 주에 샀는데, 반품을 할 거야.

A 왜? 마음에 안 들어?

B 별로. 기대했던 거하고 달라. 환불 받으려고.

104 인터넷 쇼핑 장단점

STEP 1 주제어 핵심 단어 학습 발음 / 강세 훈련

넓은 선택의 폭	a lot of options
가격을 비교하다	compare prices
최저가	lowest price
좋은 가격에 사다	get great deals
무료 배송	free shipping
허위 광고	false ad
충동구매	impulse buying
사기	fraud
배송 지연	late delivery

STEP 2 짧은 영작 연습 발음 / 강세 훈련

(1) 가격을 비교해서 최저가를 찾을 수 있어.
(compare prices / lowest price)
You can compare prices and find the lowest price.

(2) 인터넷상에서 정말 괜찮은 가격에 살 수 있어.
(get great deals)
You can get great deals on the internet.

(3) 허위 광고에 속지 않게 조심해.
(false ad)
Be careful not to fall for false ads.

STEP 3 짧은 대화 연습 발음 / 강세 훈련

A Is that the online shopping mall you mentioned?
B Yes. You can **get great deals** here.
A Really? Maybe I should check it out myself.
B You should. They have the **lowest prices**.
They also offer **free shipping**.

A 그것이 네가 언급했던 인터넷 쇼핑몰이니?
B 응. 여기서 물건 싸게 할 수 있어.
A 정말? 나도 한번 확인해봐야 겠다.
B 응, 해봐. 최저가로 살 수 있어.
배송도 무료로 해줘.

105

중고품 거래

STEP 1 주제어 핵심 단어 학습 발음 / 강세 훈련

중고품	secondhand item / used item
중고품을 구매하다	shop secondhand
멀쩡한	in good shape
양질의 제품	quality product
절반의 가격	half the price
돈을 아끼다	save money
유용하다	come in handy
재차 확인하다	double check

STEP 2 짧은 영작 연습 발음 / 강세 훈련

(1) 중고품을 사면 돈을 아낄 수 있어.
(save money / secondhand item)
You can save money if you buy a secondhand item.

(2) 그거 절반 가격에 살 수 있어.
(half the price)
You can buy it at half the price.

(3) 중고품 구매하기 전에 항상 다시 한 번 확인하는 게 좋아.
(double check / used item)
You should always double check before you buy a used item.

STEP 3 짧은 대화 연습 발음 / 강세 훈련

A I want to buy a laptop but I don't have enough money.
B Why don't you buy a secondhand item?
A That could be a good idea.
B Yeah, you can buy it at half the price. You can save money.

A 노트북 사고 싶은데, 돈이 충분하지 않아.
B 중고품 사지 그래?
A 좋은 생각일 수 있겠다.
B 응. 절반 가격에 살 수도 있어. 돈 아낄 수 있어.

매일 10분 영어 이현석의

정면돌파 스피킹

www.ebse.co.kr

여가 생활편

Exercise
운동

unit 106 ~ unit 110

106

건강 유지

STEP 1 주제어 핵심 단어 학습 발음 / 강세 훈련

운동하다	exercise / get some exercise
운동하다 / 운동	work out / workout
규칙적으로	regularly / on a regular basis
더 건강해지다	become healthier
건강/체형을 유지하다	stay in shape
체력을 유지하다	stay physically fit
유연하게 되다	become flexible
살을 빼다	lose weight

STEP 2 짧은 영작 연습 발음 / 강세 훈련

(1) 나는 규칙적으로 운동을 하려고 노력해.
(work out / on a regular basis)
I try to work out on a regular basis.

(2) 건강 유지를 위해 운동을 해야 할 거 같아.
(get some exercise / stay in shape)
I need to get some exercise to stay in shape.

(3) 운동을 하면 몸이 유연해지고 살도 뺄 수 있어.
(become flexible / lose weight)
You can become flexible and lose weight if you exercise.

STEP 3 짧은 대화 연습 발음 / 강세 훈련

A Do you **work out regularly**?

B No, not really. I feel like I need to **get some exercise** though.

A Yeah, I exercise as often as I can to **stay in shape**.

B I should do that too. I want to **lose some weight** as well.

A 너 규칙적으로 운동하니?
B 아니, 안 해. 그런데 운동을 조금 해야 할 거 같기는 해.
A 응. 나는 건강 유지하려고 최대한 자주 운동해.
B 나도 해야 하는데. 나 살도 조금 빼고 싶거든.

107

질병 예방

STEP 1 주제어 핵심 단어 학습 발음 / 강세 훈련

질병을 예방하다	prevent illnesses
만성질환 예방하다	prevent chronic diseases
체지방을 낮추다	reduce body fat
기분전환을 해주다	feel refreshed
기분을 좋게 해주다	improve one's mood
혈압을 낮추다	lower blood pressure
스트레스를 줄여주다	reduce stress
잠을 잘 오게 해주다	sleep better

STEP 2 짧은 영작 연습 발음 / 강세 훈련

(1) 운동은 여러 질병과 만성질환을 예방해준다.
(prevent illnesses / prevent chronic diseases)
Exercising prevents various illnesses and chronic diseases.

(2) 요즘 체지방을 줄이려고 노력하고 있어.
(reduce body fat)
I'm trying to reduce body fat these days.

(3) 운동을 하면 스트레스도 줄고, 잠도 더 잘 와.
(reduce stress / sleep better)
Exercising helps me reduce stress and sleep better

STEP 3 짧은 대화 연습 발음 / 강세 훈련

A You seem to be **working out** a lot these days.
B I am. I'm trying to **reduce body fat.**
A Good for you!
B **Plus,** exercising helps me **reduce stress and sleep better.**

A 너 요즘 운동 자주 하는 거 같다.
B 맞아. 체지방을 조금 줄이려고 하는 중이야.
A 멋지네!
B 더불어, 운동하면 스트레스도 줄고, 잠도 더 잘 와.

108

유산소 운동

STEP 1 주제어 핵심 단어 학습 발음 / 강세 훈련

유산소 운동	cardio exercise / aerobic exercise
유산소 운동을 하다	do some cardio
걷다	take a walk
뛰다	go for a run
자전거를 타다	ride one's bike
러닝머신	treadmill
열량을 소모하다	burn calories
혈액순환을 촉진하다	facilitate blood circulation
신진대사를 촉진하다	increase one's metabolism

STEP 2 짧은 영작 연습 발음 / 강세 훈련

(1) 유산소 운동을 매일 한 시간씩 하고 있어.
(do some cardio)
I do some cardio for an hour every day.

(2) 나 이따 저녁에 조금 뛰고 오려고.
(go for a run)
I'm going to go for a run later in the evening.

(3) 자전거 타는 것은 열량 소모에 도움이 된다.
(ride one's bike / burn calories)
Riding my bike helps me burn some calories.

STEP 3 짧은 대화 연습 발음 / 강세 훈련

A Do you **do some cardio** every time you work out?
B Yes, I run on the **treadmill** for an hour.
A Does it help?
B Yes, it helps me **burn some calories.**
It also **increases my metabolism.**

A 운동할 때마다 유산소 운동 하니?
B 응. 한 시간 동안 러닝머신 위에서 뛰어.
A 도움이 돼?
B 응. 열량 소모에 도움이 돼.
신진대사도 촉진시켜 주고.

109

근력 운동

STEP 1 **주제어 핵심 단어 학습** 발음 / 강세 훈련

근육	muscles
근육질인	muscular
웨이트 트레이닝을 하다	lift weights
윗몸 일으키기	sit-ups
팔 굽혀 펴기	push-ups
턱걸이	pull-ups
허리 근육	back muscles
어깨 근육	shoulder muscles
복근	abs (abdominal muscles)

STEP 2 짧은 영작 연습 발음 / 강세 훈련

(1) 운동할 때 웨이트 트레이닝도 하니?

(lift weights)

Do you lift weights when you work out?

(2) 윗몸 일으키기하고 팔 굽혀 펴기 매일 하고 있어.

(sit-ups / push-ups)

I am doing sit-ups and push-ups every day.

(3) 나 복근 운동을 많이 하고 있어.

(abs)

I'm working on my abs a lot.

STEP 3 짧은 대화 연습 발음 / 강세 훈련

A Do you **lift weights** when you work out?

B Yes, I'm working on my **back muscles**.

A Is there a reason you are doing that?

B I have back pain quite often,
so I have to strengthen my **back muscles**.

A 운동할 때 웨이트 트레이닝도 하니?

B 응. 허리 근육 운동하고 있어.

A 그렇게 하는 이유가 있니?

B 응. 허리가 제법 자주 아파서, 허리 근육을 강화해야 해.

110 헬스/요가

STEP 1 주제어 핵심 단어 학습 발음 / 강세 훈련

헬스클럽	gym / fitness center
트레이너	personal trainer
트레이닝 수업	training session
요가 수업을 듣다	take yoga classes
요가 강습소	yoga studio
필라테스 강습을 받다	take pilates lessons
크로스핏 강습	cross-fit classes
근육을 스트레칭하다	stretch one's muscles
마사지를 받다	get a massage
자세를 교정하다	adjust one's posture

STEP 2 짧은 영작 연습 발음 / 강세 훈련

(1) 나 오늘 트레이너하고 운동 잡혀 있어.
(training session / personal trainer)
I have a training session with my personal trainer today.

(2) 요즘 요가 배우는 사람들이 정말 많아.
(take yoga classes)
There are many people who take yoga classes these days.

(3) 나 필라테스 강습 받아볼까 생각 중이야.
(take pilates lessons)
I'm thinking of taking pilates lessons.

STEP 3 짧은 대화 연습 발음 / 강세 훈련

A Many of my friends **take yoga classes.**

B Yeah, yoga has become very common these days.

A There are many people who **take pilates lessons** as well.

B I know. There are **pilates studios** all over the place.

A 내 친구 중에 요가 배우는 친구들이 많아.
B 응. 요즘 요가가 정말 보편화 되었어.
A 필라테스 강습 받는 사람들도 많아.
B 알아. 사방에 필라테스 강습소들 본 거 같아.

매일 10분 영어 이현석의

정면돌파 스피킹

www.ebse.co.kr

여가 생활편

Friends
친구

unit 111 ~ unit 115

unit 111. 학창 시절 친구

unit 112. 고마운 친구

unit 113. 친구 연락

unit 114. 친구 모임

unit 115. 싸움/화해

111

학창 시절 친구

STEP 1 주제어 핵심 단어 학습 발음 / 강세 훈련

학창시절 친구	a friend back from school
오래된 친구	an old friend
친한 친구	a close friend
고등학교 친구	high school buddy
즐거웠던 추억	enjoyable memories
좋았던 시절이 그립다	miss the good old days
오래전부터 알고 지내다	go a long way back
같은 반이었다	be in the same class
매우 가까운 사이이다	be very tight

STEP 2 짧은 영작 연습 발음 / 강세 훈련

(1) 그 친구는 학창시절 친구야.

(a friend back from school)

She is a friend back from school.

(2) 그 친구하고 나는 오래전부터 알고 지내온 사이야.

(go a long way back)

He and I go a long way back.

(3) 우리는 고등학교 내내 같은 반이었어.

(be in the same class)

We were in the same class through out high school.

STEP 3 짧은 대화 연습 발음 / 강세 훈련

A Is she **a friend back from school**?

B Yes, she and I **go a long way back**.

A Were you guys close?

B Uh-huh. We were best friends.
Oh, I **miss the good old days**.

A 그 친구 학창시절 친구니?

B 응. 그 친구하고 나는 오래전부터 알고 지내온 사이야.

A 친한 사이였니?

B 응. 가장 친한 친구였어. 아, 좋았던 그 시절이 그립다.

112

고마운 친구

STEP 1 주제어 핵심 단어 학습 발음 / 강세 훈련

우정	friendship
고마운	thankful
감사하게 여기는	grateful
축복	blessing
의지하다	rely on / depend on
지지해주는	supportive
용기를 주다	encourage
기분을 좋게 해주다	cheer me up
내 편이 되어주다	be on my side

STEP 2 짧은 영작 연습 발음 / 강세 훈련

(1) 나는 그런 친구가 있어서 정말 감사하게 생각해.
(grateful)
I really feel grateful that I have a friend like him.

(2) 그 친구는 내가 하는 일을 항상 지지해줘.
(supportive)
She is very supportive of what I do.

(3) 그는 나를 항상 응원해주고 기분 좋게 해줘.
(encourage / cheer me up)
He always encourages me and cheers me up.

STEP 3 짧은 대화 연습 발음 / 강세 훈련

A You guys seem to be very close.
B Yeah, I'm **grateful** that I have a friend like him.
A That's good to know.
B He always **encourages** me and **cheers me up**.

A 너희들 정말 친해 보인다.
B 응. 저런 친구가 있다는 게 감사할 뿐이야.
A 그거 다행이네.
B 나를 항상 응원해주고 기분 좋게 해줘.

113

친구 연락

STEP 1 주제어 핵심 단어 학습 발음 / 강세 훈련

연락하며 지내다	keep in touch / stay in touch
연락이 끊기다	fall out of touch
안부를 확인하다	check up on
서로 안부를 묻다	ask how each other is doing
밀린 이야기를 하다	do some catching up
서로 전화를 하다	call each other
전화를 걸다	give someone a ring
이야기를 하다	chat with someone
메시지를 주고 받다	send messages back and forth

STEP 2 짧은 영작 연습 발음 / 강세 훈련

(1) 너희들 서로 연락하고 지내니?
(keep in touch)
Do you guys keep in touch?

(2) 우리는 서로 안부를 묻고 밀린 이야기를 했어.
(do some catching up)
We asked how each other is doing and did some catching up

(3) 우리는 자주 메시지를 주고 받아.
(send messages back and forth)
We often send messages back and forth.

STEP 3 짧은 대화 연습 발음 / 강세 훈련

A Do you guys keep in touch?
B Oh, yes! We send messages back and forth quite often.
A I see. When the last time you guys met?
B I think it was a month ago.
We did a lot of catching up

A 너희들 연락하며 지내니?
B 그럼! 서로 메시지 제법 자주 주고 받는 편이야.
A 그렇구나. 마지막으로 만난 게 언제니?
B 한 달 전이었던 거 같아. 서로 밀린 이야기를 많이 했어.

114

친구 모임

STEP 1 주제어 핵심 단어 학습 발음 / 강세 훈련

모이다	gather / get together
모임	gathering / get-together
동문회	school reunion
특별한 게재	special occasion
얼굴 보다	touch base
뜻 깊은 시간을 보내다	spend some quality time
커피를 마시면서 이야기하다	chat over coffee
~에게 저녁식사를 대접하다	take someone out for dinner

STEP 2 짧은 영작 연습 발음 / 강세 훈련

(1) 나 어제 친구들 모임이 있었어.
(gathering)
I have a gathering with my friends yesterday.

(2) 나 다음 주에 학교 동문회가 있어.
(school reunion)
I have a school reunion next week.

(3) 우리 얼굴을 본 지 꽤 시간이 됐어.
(touch base)
It's been quite a while since we touched base.

STEP 3 짧은 대화 연습 발음 / 강세 훈련

A Do you have any plans for the weekend?
B I'm **getting together** with my friends.
A Oh, really? Is it a **special occasion**?
B No, it's just a casual **gathering**.
We **haven't touched base** for a while.

A 주말에 계획 있니?
B 친구들하고 모일 예정이야.
A 아, 정말? 특별한 게재니?
B 아니, 그냥 편한 모임 자리야. 서로 얼굴을 본 지 제법 오래 되어서.

115 싸움/화해

STEP 1 주제어 핵심 단어 학습 발음 / 강세 훈련

오해	misunderstanding
싸우다	have a fight / have an argument
서로 잘 지내지 못하다	not get along
화해하다	make up
사과하다	apologize
진정성 있는 사과	sincere apology
좋은 관계를 유지하다	be on good terms
상처를 주다	hurt one's feelings

STEP 2 짧은 영작 연습 발음 / 강세 훈련

(1) 나 그 친구하고 크게 싸웠어.
(have a fight)
I had a big fight with him.

(2) 우리는 결국 화해를 했어.
(make up)
We eventually made up.

(3) 서로 사과를 했고 이제는 잘 지내고 있어.
(apologize / be on good terms)
We apologized to each other and we are on good terms now.

STEP 3 짧은 대화 연습 발음 / 강세 훈련

A Did you guys **have a fight**?
B Yeah, we had a **misunderstanding**.
A Really? Did you guys **make up**?
B Uh-huh. I apologized to her and we **are on good terms** now.

A 너희들 싸웠니?
B 응. 서로 오해가 있었어.
A 정말? 서로 화해는 했니?
B 응. 그 친구한테 내가 사과했고, 이제는 잘 지내고 있어.

매일 10분 영어 이현석의

정면돌파 스피킹

www.ebse.co.kr

여가 생활편

Restaurants
음식점

unit 116 ~ unit 120

116

음식점 종류

STEP 1 주제어 핵심 단어 학습 발음 / 강세 훈련

한국 음식점	Korean restaurant
일식당	Japanese restaurant
태국 음식점	Thai place
베트남 음식점	Vietnamese place
패스트푸드 체인점	fast food chain
햄버거점	burger joint
뷔페 식당	buffet restaurant
동네 식당	local restaurant
근사한 식당	fancy restaurant
괜찮은 식당	decent restaurant

STEP 2 짧은 영작 연습 발음 / 강세 훈련

(1) 내가 정말 좋아하는 베트남 음식점이 있어.
(Vietnamese place)
There is a Vietnamese place I really like.

(2) 우리는 그냥 동네 음식점에서 저녁을 먹었어.
(local restaurant)
We just had dinner at a local restaurant.

(3) 우리 회사 근처에 괜찮은 음식점이 많아.
(decent restaurant)
There are many decent restaurants near my office.

STEP 3 짧은 대화 연습 발음 / 강세 훈련

A So, where do you want to eat?
B There are many **decent restaurants** nearby.
A Great. Which is a favorite place?
B There is a **fancy Thai place** right around the corner. Let's go there.

A 어디 가서 먹을까?
B 이 근처에 괜찮은 식당들이 많아.
A 잘 됐네. 가장 좋아하는 곳이 어디니?
B 바로 근처에 근사한 태국 식당이 하나 있어. 거기 가자.

117 음식점 메뉴

STEP 1 주제어 핵심 단어 학습 발음 / 강세 훈련

메뉴판	menu
바비큐	barbeque
국	soup
찌개	stew
요리	cuisine
메인 요리	main dish
사이드 요리	side dish
에피타이저	appetizer
후식	dessert
코스 요리	course meal

STEP 2 짧은 영작 연습 발음 / 강세 훈련

(1) 메뉴 좀 가져다 주시겠어요?

(menu)

Can I get the menu, please?

(2) 거기에서 맛있는 현지 요리들을 먹었어.

(cuisine)

I tried a lot of delicious local cuisine there.

(3) 메인 요리가 나오기 전에 에피타이저가 나왔어.

(appetizer / main dish)

They brought us an appetizer before the main dish.

STEP 3 짧은 대화 연습 발음 / 강세 훈련

A There's so many items on the **menu.**

B I know. I have no clue what to order.

A Why don't we start with an **appetizer**?

B Good idea. We can ask for recommendations for the **main dish.**

A 메뉴판에 음식 종류가 정말 많다.

B 그러게. 뭘 시켜야 할지 도통 모르겠다.

A 에피타이저부터 시작하면 어떨까?

B 좋은 생각이네. 메인 요리는 추천해달라고 하자.

118

음식점 계산

STEP 1 주제어 핵심 단어 학습 발음 / 강세 훈련

밥값을 내다	pay for one's meal
나눠서 내다	split the bill
계산을 하다	get the bill
내가 내다	be on me
신용카드로 결제하다	pay with one's credit card
현금 결제하다	pay in cash
가격이 합리적인	reasonable
제법 비싼	pricey

STEP 2 짧은 영작 연습 발음 / 강세 훈련

(1) 오늘은 제가 낼게요.
(get the bill / be on me)
Let me get the bill today. / This is on me.

(2) 우리 나눠서 계산할까요?
(split the bill)
Should we split the bill?

(3) 요즘에는 거의 현금을 결제하는 경우가 없어.
(pay in cash)
I rarely pay in cash these days.

STEP 3 짧은 대화 연습 발음 / 강세 훈련

A Let me **get the bill** today.
B No, no*!* It's my turn to pay. Give me the **bill***!*
A We ate a lot today though.
Let's **split the bill** then.
B No, I insist*!* Please let me pay this time.

A 오늘은 내가 낼게.
B 아니야*!* 내가 낼 차례야. 계산서 줘.
A 오늘 우리 많이 먹었어. 그럼 나눠서 내자.
B 아니야, 내 말 대로 해줘. 이번에는 내가 낼게.

119 음식점 검색

STEP 1 주제어 핵심 단어 학습 발음 / 강세 훈련

인터넷 검색하다	do an online search
음식점을 검색하다	search for a restaurant
고객 후기	customer review
찾아 가는 길	directions
영업 시간	business hours
늦게까지 영업하다	open until late
일찍 영업을 종료하다	close early
연중무휴	24/7
예약을 하다	make a reservation

STEP 2 짧은 영작 연습 발음 / 강세 훈련

(1) 음식점 검색해보자.
(do an online search)
Let's do an online search for a place to eat.

(2) 거기 찾아가는 방법 좀 알려주시겠어요?
(directions)
Can you give me some directions to that place?

(3) 넌 예약을 미리 해야 돼.
(make a reservation)
You have to make a reservation in advance.

STEP 3 짧은 대화 연습 발음 / 강세 훈련

A I **made a reservation** at that restaurant.

B Good, but I don't know how to get there.
Can you give me some **directions**?

A Just punch the name of the restaurant in the GPS.

B Got it!

A 그 식당에 예약했어.
B 좋아, 그런데 나 가는 방법 몰라. 찾아 가는 방법 좀 알려줘.
A 그냥 식당 이름 네비게이션에 쳐.
B 알았어.

120

음식 배달/테이크아웃

STEP 1 주제어 핵심 단어 학습 발음 / 강세 훈련

배달 음식점	delivery restaurant
시켜 먹다	order in
음식을 배달시키다	have food delivered
테이크아웃 음식점	take-out place
테이크아웃하다	get the food to go
음식 배달앱	food delivery app
곧장 결제하다	pay directly
배달 주소	delivery address
도착 예상시간	ETA (estimated time of arrival)

STEP 2 짧은 영작 연습 발음 / 강세 훈련

(1) 우리 오늘 그냥 시켜 먹는 것이 어떠니?
(order in)
Why don't we just order in today?

(2) 음식 포장해서 나가는 거 어떨까?
(get the food to go)
Should we just get the food to go?

(3) 앱에 배달 주소가 이미 저장되어 있어.
(delivery address)
The delivery address is stored on the app.

STEP 3 짧은 대화 연습 발음 / 강세 훈련

A Why don't we just **order in** today?
B Sure, why not? Are you going to use that **food delivery app**?
A Uh-huh. It's so easy to **have food delivered** these days.
B I know. The app also gives you the **ETA**.

A 오늘은 그냥 시켜 먹으면 어떨까?
B 그래, 그러자. 그 음식 배달앱 쓸 거니?
A 응. 요즘은 음식 시켜 먹는 것이 너무 쉬워졌어.
B 알아. 앱에서 음식 도착예정 시간도 알려주잖아. .

매일 10분 영어 이현석의

정면돌파 스피킹

www.ebse.co.kr

여가 생활편

Coffee Shops
커피

unit 121 ~ unit 125

unit 121. 커피숍 종류

unit 122. 커피숍 메뉴

unit 123. 커피숍 위치

unit 124. 커피숍 주문

unit 125. 커피숍 가격

121

커피숍 종류

STEP 1 주제어 핵심 단어 학습 발음 / 강세 훈련

커피숍	coffee shop / coffee house
커피 전문점	coffee place
동네 카페	local cafe
전국 체인망	national chain
전 세계적인 체인망	international chain
지점	branch
테이크아웃점	take-out place
일회용컵	disposable cup
빨대	straw

STEP 2 짧은 영작 연습 발음 / 강세 훈련

(1) 내가 자주 가는 동네 카페가 있어요.
(local cafe)
There is a local cafe I go to often.

(2) 나 그 커피숍 단골이야.
(coffee place)
I am a regular at that coffee place.

(3) 이 커피숍은 전국 체인점이야.
(national chain)
This coffee shop is a national chain.

STEP 3 짧은 대화 연습 발음 / 강세 훈련

A There is a coffee shop I go to quite often.
B Is it a national chain?
A No, it's a local cafe.
I am a regular at that place.
B Does their coffee taste good?

A 내가 제법 자주 가는 커피숍이 하나 있어.
B 전국 체인점이야?
A 아니, 그냥 동네 커피숍이야. 나 거기 단골이야.
B 거기 커피 맛이 있니?

122

커피숍 메뉴

STEP 1 주제어 핵심 단어 학습 발음 / 강세 훈련

아메리카노	americano
라떼	latte
에스프레소	espresso
카푸치노	cappuccino
더블샷	double shot
스무디	smoothie
아이스 커피	iced coffee
갓 내린 커피	freshly brewed coffee
핸드 드립 커피	hand-dripped coffee
인스턴트 커피	instant coffee

STEP 2 짧은 영작 연습 발음 / 강세 훈련

(1) 나는 항상 아메리카노만 주문해.

(americano)

I always order an americano.

(2) 아이스 커피 마실 거니?

(iced coffee)

Are you going to have an iced coffee?

(3) 나는 매일 아침마다 갓 내린 커피를 마시는 걸 좋아 해.

(freshly brewed coffee)

I like to have freshly brewed coffee every morning.

STEP 3 짧은 대화 연습 발음 / 강세 훈련

A What kind of **coffee** do you like?

B I always order an **americano.**

A Hot or cold?

B I like my coffee hot.
I have **freshly brewed coffee** every morning.

A 커피 무슨 종류 좋아하니?
B 나는 항상 아메리카노 주문해.
A 뜨거운 거, 차가운 거?
B 난 커피 뜨겁게 마시는 거 좋아해. 나는 매일 아침마다 갓 내린 커피 마셔.

123

커피숍 위치

STEP 1 주제어 핵심 단어 학습 발음 / 강세 훈련

번화가	on busy streets
거리마다	on every street corner
사방에	all over the place
전국에	all across the country
전 세계에	all around the world
가깝다	be close by
근처에	nearby
바로 근처에	just around the corner
길 건너 편에	across the street
아랫층에 / 윗층에	downstairs / upstairs

STEP 2 짧은 영작 연습 발음 / 강세 훈련

(1) 요즘에는 사방에 커피숍들이 있는 거 같아.
(all over the place)
Coffee shops are all over the place these days.

(2) 길 건너편에 작은 카페 하나 있어.
(across the street)
There is a small cafe across the street.

(3) 아랫층에 커피숍들 여러 개 있어.
(downstairs)
There are several coffee places downstairs.

STEP 3 짧은 대화 연습 발음 / 강세 훈련

A There are coffee shops **all over the place**. Which one should we go to?
B There is a nice cafe **across the street**.
A Is it **nearby**?
B Yes, it's only a five-minute walk.

A 사방에 다 커피숍이네. 어느 곳에 갈까?
B 길 건너 편에 괜찮은 곳이 있어.
A 가깝니?
B 응. 걸어서 5분 거리야.

124

커피숍 주문

STEP 1 주제어 핵심 단어 학습 발음 / 강세 훈련

주문하다	order
주문을 하다	make one's order
주문을 바꾸다	change one's order
주문을 취소하다	cancel one's order
무엇을 시킬지 정하다	decide what to get
줄을 서다	stand in line
줄을 서서 기다리다	wait in line
진동벨	buzzer
카페인	caffeine
카페인 없는	de-caf (decaffeinated)

STEP 2 짧은 영작 연습 발음 / 강세 훈련

(1) 무엇을 시킬지 정했니?

(decide what to get)

Have you decided what to get?

(2) 나 주문 바꿔도 되는지 물어 봐야겠다.

(change one's order)

I'm going to ask if I can change one's order.

(3) 줄 서서 우리 차례를 기다려야 돼.

(wait in line)

We have to wait in line for our turn.

STEP 3 짧은 대화 연습 발음 / 강세 훈련

A Wow! Look at that long line.

B I know. We have to **wait in line** for our turn.

A Have you **decided what to get**?

B Not yet. I'm going to take a look at the menu.

A 우와! 저 긴 줄 좀 봐.
B 알아. 차례 기다리기 위해 줄 서서 기다려야 겠네.
A 뭐 시킬지 정했니?
B 아직. 메뉴 보고 정하려고.

125

커피숍 가격

STEP 1 주제어 핵심 단어 학습 발음 / 강세 훈련

비싼	expensive
가격이 부담이 되는	pricey
가격이 너무 높은	over-priced
가격이 싼	cheap
가격이 합리적인	reasonable
할인을 받다	get a discount
음료를 무료로 받다	get a free drink
상품권	gift voucher

STEP 2 짧은 영작 연습 발음 / 강세 훈련

(1) 일부 커피숍 음료 가격이 너무 비싼 거 같아.
(over-priced)
I think drinks at some coffee shops are over-priced.

(2) 거기 카페 음료 가격이 합리적인 편이야.
(reasonable)
The prices at that cafe are reasonable.

(3) 나 이 커피 상품권 써서 음료 무료로 받을 거야.
(get a free drink / gift voucher)
I'm going to use this gift voucher to get a free drink.

STEP 3 짧은 대화 연습 발음 / 강세 훈련

A Coffee is **expensive** here.

B Yeah, I think they are a bit **over-priced.**

A It doesn't matter. I'm going to use this **gift voucher to get a free drink.**

B Where did you get that?

A 여기 커피 비싸.
B 알아. 너무 가격이 비싼 거 같기는 해.
A 상관 없어. 나 이 커피 상품권 써서 음료 무료로 받을 거야.
B 그거 어디서 났어?

매일 10분 영어 이현석의

정면돌파 스피킹

www.ebse.co.kr

여가 생활편

Alcohol
주류

unit 126 ~ unit 130

126

술 종류

STEP 1 주제어 핵심 단어 학습 발음 / 강세 훈련

술을 마시다	have a drink
한잔하다	grab a drink
병맥주	bottled beer
생맥주	draft beer
수제맥주	craft beer
국산맥주	domestic beer
수입맥주	imported beer
양주	hard liquor
화이트 와인	white wine
레드 와인	red wine
막걸리/동동주	Korean rice wine

STEP 2 짧은 영작 연습 발음 / 강세 훈련

(1) 병맥주 좋아하세요, 생맥주 좋아하세요?
(bottled beer / draft beer)
Do you like draft beer or draft beer?

(2) 전 세계 각지에서 들어온 다양한 수입맥주가 있습니다.
(imported beer)
There are various types of imported beer from all across the world.

(3) 나 화이트 와인 마시고 싶어.
(white wine)
I'm in the mood for some white wine.

STEP 3 짧은 대화 연습 발음 / 강세 훈련

A Do you want to **grab a drink**?

B Sure. I'm in the mood for some **beer**.

A What kind of beer do you like?

B I'll just have some **draft beer**.
Let's see what they have on the menu.

A 술 한잔 할까?
B 응. 나 맥주 한잔 마시고 싶어.
A 무슨 맥주 마시고 싶어?
B 그냥 생맥주 마시지 뭐. 메뉴판에 뭐 있나 한번 보자.

127

술안주

STEP 1 주제어 핵심 단어 학습 발음 / 강세 훈련

잘 어울리다	go well with
치킨	fried chicken
양념치킨	marinated fried chicken
해산물	seafood
회	raw fish
게	crab
새우	shrimp
구이	barbeque
돼지고기 / 소고기	pork / beef
오리고기 / 양고기	duck / lamb
찌개	stew

STEP 2 짧은 영작 연습 발음 / 강세 훈련

(1) 치킨은 맥주와 정말 잘 어울린다.

(go well with)

Fried chicken really goes well with beer.

(2) 술과 함께 회와 구운 새우를 먹었습니다.

(raw fish / shrimp)

We had raw fish and grilled shrimp with the drinks.

(3) 찌개와 같이 술을 마시면 덜 취하는 거 같다.

(stew)

I think I get less drunk when I have drinks with stews.

STEP 3 짧은 대화 연습 발음 / 강세 훈련

A What do you like to have with beer?

B Well, I think **fried chicken goes well with beer**.

A I agree. They are a perfect match.

B Speaking of which, why don't we order some chicken now?

A 맥주하고 같이 무슨 안주 먹는 거 좋아하니?
B 글쎄, 치킨이 맥주하고 가장 잘 어울리는 거 같아.
A 맞아. 환상의 궁합이지.
B 말이 나와 말인데, 우리 지금 치킨 시킬까?

128

술집

STEP 1 주제어 핵심 단어 학습 발음 / 강세 훈련

한국 술집	Korean bar
웨스턴 바	Western bar
일본식 선술집	Japanese bar
호프집	pub
맥주집	beer place
맥주 체인점	beer chain
치킨 체인점	chicken chain
근사한 술집	fancy bar
동네 술집	local bar

STEP 2 짧은 영작 연습 발음 / 강세 훈련

(1) 이 근처에 내가 좋아하는 맥주집 있어.
(beer place)
There is a beer place I like near here.

(2) 이 곳이 유명한 맥주 체인점인지 몰랐어.
(beer chain)
I didn't know this place was a famous beer chain.

(3) 나 동네 술집 한 군데에 단골이야.
(local bar)
I'm a regular at a local bar.

STEP 3 짧은 대화 연습 발음 / 강세 훈련

A Do you have a bar you go to often?
B Yes, I'm a regular at a local bar.
A What kind of place is it?
B It's just a typical beer chain.
I like the mood there.

A 자주 가는 술집 있니?
B 응, 동네 술집 한 군데에 단골이야.
A 어떤 종류의 술집인데?
B 그냥 평범한 맥주 체인점이야. 거기 분위기가 좋아.

129

과음

STEP 1 주제어 핵심 단어 학습 발음 / 강세 훈련

취하다	get drunk / be drunk
알딸딸하다	feel tipsy
취기가 돌다	have a buzz
만취가 되다	get wasted
비틀거리다	cannot walk straight
필름이 끊기다	black out
잠이 들다	fall asleep
실수를 하다	make a mistake
분란을 일으키다	cause trouble
중요한 물건을 분실하다	lose something important

STEP 2 짧은 영작 연습 발음 / 강세 훈련

(1) 나 벌써 알딸딸하고 제대로 못 걷겠어.

(feel tipsy / cannot walk straight)

I feel tipsy already and cannot walk straight.

(2) 나 어젯밤에 만취가 되어서 기억이 안 나.

(get wasted / black out)

I got wasted and blacked out last night.

(3) 나는 취해서 창피한 실수를 했어.

(make a mistake)

I made an embarrassing mistake because I was drunk.

STEP 3 짧은 대화 연습 발음 / 강세 훈련

A You look a little tired today.

B I drank a lot last night. I fell asleep at the bar.

A Oh, no! Was it that bad?

B Uh-huh. I got wasted and blacked out.

A 너 오늘 약간 피곤해 보인다.
B 어제 저녁에 술을 많이 마셨어. 술집에서 잠까지 들었어.
A 이런! 그 정도로 심했어?
B 응. 만취가 되어서 기억이 잘 안나.

128

숙취

STEP 1 주제어 핵심 단어 학습 발음 / 강세 훈련

숙취가 있다	have a hangover
숙취 해소 약	hangover relief medication
숙취 해소 음료	hangover relief drink
해장국	hangover relief soup
숙취가 있다	be hung over
두통이 심하게 있다	have a splitting headache
속이 울렁거리다	feel like throwing up
물을 자꾸 먹게 되다	feel dehydrated
술이 깨다	sober up

STEP 2 짧은 영작 연습 발음 / 강세 훈련

(1) 나 숙취가 정말 심해.

(have a hangover)

I have a terrible hangover.

(2) 머리가 너무 아프고, 속이 울렁거려.

(have a splitting headache

I have a splitting headache and feel like throwing up.

(3) 술이 깨는데 시간이 제법 오래 걸렸어.

(sober up)

It took me quite a while to sober up.

STEP 3 짧은 대화 연습 발음 / 강세 훈련

A **I am so hung over.**

B **Me, too. I have a terrible hangover.**

A **I have a splitting headache.**

B **It's going to take us a while sober up.**

A 나 숙취가 너무 심해.

B 나도. 숙취가 극심하네.

A 머리가 빠개질 거처럼 아파.

B 우리 술 깨는데 시간이 좀 걸릴 거야.

매일 10분 영어 이현석의

정면돌파 스피킹

www.ebse.co.kr

여가 생활편

Gatherings
모임

unit 131 ~ unit 135

131 모임 종류

STEP 1 주제어 핵심 단어 학습 발음 / 강세 훈련

친구 모임	social gathering
가족 모임	family gathering
모임	get-together
회식	staff dinner
뒤풀이	after-party
생일	birthday party
집들이	housewarming party
송년회	year-end party
환영회	welcome party
송별회	farewell party
기념일	anniversary

STEP 2 짧은 영작 연습 발음 / 강세 훈련

(1) 이번 주말에 가족 모임이 있어요.
(family gathering)
I have a family gathering this weekend.

(2) 나 집들이를 할까 생각 중이야.
(housewarming party)
I'm thinking of holding a housewarming party.

(3) 그를 위해서 마지막날 우리가 송별회를 해줬어.
(farewell party)
We had a farewell party for him on his last day.

STEP 3 짧은 대화 연습 발음 / 강세 훈련

A We have **staff-dinner** tonight. Are you coming?
B No, I have a **family gathering**.
A Oh, okay. Maybe next time then.
B Yeah, I feel bad about not being able to go.

A 오늘 저녁에 직원 회식 있는데. 너 참석하니?
B 아니, 나 가족 모임이 있어.
A 아, 그렇구나. 다음에 와 그럼.
B 응. 못 가게 되어서 조금 미안한 마음이 드네.

132 모임 계획

STEP 1 주제어 핵심 단어 학습 발음 / 강세 훈련

파티를 열다	throw a party
모임을 주선하다	organize a gathering
주선자	organizer
장소와 시간	time and place
장소	venue
날짜	date
누구를 초대할지	who to invite
어떻게 초대할지	how to invite people
초대장	invitation
참석 여부 회신	RSVP

STEP 2 짧은 영작 연습 발음 / 강세 훈련

(1) 나는 모임을 자주 주선하는 편이야.
(organize a gathering)
I organize gatherings quite often.

(2) 가장 좋은 시간과 장소가 어떻게 되지?
(time and place)
What is the best time and place for our gathering?

(3) 모임에 누구 초대할지 정했니?
(who to invite)
Have you decided who to invite to the gathering?

STEP 3 짧은 대화 연습 발음 / 강세 훈련

A Have you decided **who to invite** to the party?
B Not yet. It has been a while since I **organized a gathering** like this.
A Do you need any help?
B Thanks, but I think I can do it myself.

A 파티에 누구 초대할지 정했니?
B 아직. 이런 모임 주선해본 지 조금 오래 되어서.
A 뭐 도와줄까?
B 고마운데, 나 혼자 할 수 있을 거 같아.

133

모임 비용

STEP 1 주제어 핵심 단어 학습 발음 / 강세 훈련

비용	cost
비용을 충당하다	cover the cost
비용을 분담하다	share the cost
균등하게 나눠서 내다	split the bill evenly
예산을 확정하다	set the budget
예산을 넘어가다	go over the budget
돈이 남다	have some money left
돈이 모자라다	be short on money

STEP 2 짧은 영작 연습 발음 / 강세 훈련

(1) 우리 이번 모임 비용은 어떻게 처리할꺼니?
(cover the cost)
How are we going to cover the cost for the gathering?

(2) 정해 놓은 예산을 넘어가지 않게 주의해.
(go over the budget)
Be careful not to go over the budget.

(3) 지난번 모임에서 남은 돈이 조금 있어.
(have some money left)
We have some money left from our last gathering.

STEP 3 짧은 대화 연습 발음 / 강세 훈련

A **How are we going to cover the cost for the gathering?**
B **We need to set the budget.**
A **Let's do it right this time.**
B **Uh-huh. We went over the budget last time.**

A 이번 모임 비용 처리 어떻게 할꺼니?
B 예산을 잡아야 해.
A 이번에는 제대로 해보자.
B 응. 지난번에는 예산을 넘어갔잖아.

134 모임 빈도

STEP 1 주제어 핵심 단어 학습 발음 / 강세 훈련

매우 자주	frequently
주기적으로	regularly
때때로	from time to time
가끔씩	every now and then
종종	off and on
매월	every month
격월로	every other month
무작위로	randomly
최대한 자주	as often as we can
할 수 있을 때마다	whenever we can
기회가 있을 때마다	whenever we have the chance

STEP 2 짧은 영작 연습 발음 / 강세 훈련

(1) 나는 학교 친구들을 종종 만난다.
(off and on)
I meet up with my school friends off and on.

(2) 우리는 그냥 번개를 해서 만나는 경우가 많아.
(randomly)
We just get together randomly.

(3) 우리는 기회가 있을 때마다 모임을 가져.
(whenever we have the chance)
We have gatherings whenever we have the chance.

STEP 3 짧은 대화 연습 발음 / 강세 훈련

A How often do you meet up with your friends?
B Well, we just get together randomly.
A Don't you have any regular get-togethers?
B No, we just meet up off and on.

A 친구들 얼마나 자주 만나는 편이니?
B 글쎄, 그냥 상황에 따라 보는 거 같아.
A 정기적으로 하는 모임 없어?
B 없어. 그냥 대중 없이 종종 만나.

135

모임 추억

STEP 1 주제어 핵심 단어 학습 발음 / 강세 훈련

되돌아보다	look back on
회상하다	reflect on
인상깊은	memorable
즐거운	enjoyable
흥겨운	delighted
잊을 수 없는	unforgettable
끔찍한	awful
창피한	embarrassing
어색한	awkward

STEP 2 짧은 영작 연습 발음 / 강세 훈련

(1) 정말 기억에 남는 모임이었어.
(memorable)
It was a very memorable gathering.

(2) 우리 모두 서로 얼굴을 봐서 신이 났어.
(delighted)
We were all delighted to see each other.

(3) 처음에는 다들 서로 조금 어색해 했어.
(awkward)
We all felt a little awkward at first.

STEP 3 짧은 대화 연습 발음 / 강세 훈련

A Do you remember the last gathering we had?
B How could I forget that?
It was quite **memorable.**
A I know. We had so much fun.
B Yeah, it was an **unforgettable** gathering.

A 우리 지난번에 했던 모임 기억나?
B 그것을 어떻게 잊어? 정말 기억에 남아.
A 맞아. 정말 재미 있었어.
B 응. 정말 잊을 수 없는 모임이었어.

여가 생활편

Holidays
휴일

unit 136 ~ unit 140

136

공휴일

STEP 1 주제어 핵심 단어 학습 발음 / 강세 훈련

공휴일	public holiday
삼일절	Independence Movement Day
석가탄신일	Buddha's Birthday
현충일	Memorial Day
어린이 날	Children's Day
광복절	Independence Day / Liberation Day
개천절	National Foundation Day
크리스마스	Christmas
대체휴일	substitute holiday

STEP 2 짧은 영작 연습 발음 / 강세 훈련

(1) 이번 달에 공휴일이 두 개나 있어.
(public holiday)
We have two public holidays this month.

(2) 현충일에 뭐 할 거니?
(Memorial Day)
What are you doing on Memorial Day?

(3) 월요일이 대체휴일로 지정되었어.
(substitute holiday)
Monday was designated as a substitute holiday.

STEP 3 짧은 대화 연습 발음 / 강세 훈련

A We have a **public holiday** this week.
It's **Independence Day**.

B Yes, it's Thursday. I'm going take an extra day off on Friday.

A Wow! You will have a long holiday then.

B Many of my co-workers are doing the same thing.

A 이번 주에 공휴일이 있어. 광복절이야.
B 응. 목요일이야. 나 금요일에 하루를 추가로 휴가 낼 거야.
A 우와! 그럼 긴 연휴가 되겠네.
B 내 동료 중에도 그렇게 하는 사람 많아.

137

명절

STEP 1 주제어 핵심 단어 학습 발음 / 강세 훈련

전통 명절	family holiday
설 명절	Korean New Year's Holiday
추석 명절	Korean Thanksgiving Holiday
친척들과 모이다	get together with relatives
명절 음식을 하다	cook holiday food
선물을 교환하다	exchange gifts
차례를 지내다	hold traditional memorials
성묘를 가다	visit ancestors' graves
예를 표하다	pay our respects

STEP 2 짧은 영작 연습 발음 / 강세 훈련

(1) 한국에는 큰 명절이 두 개가 있다.
(family holiday)
There are two family holidays in Korea.

(2) 우리는 친척들과 한자리에 모일 예정이야.
(get together with relatives)
We are going to get together with our relatives

(3) 우리는 같이 명절 음식을 하고 선물을 서로 주고 받아.
(cook holiday food / exchange gifts)
We cook holiday food together and exchange gifts.

STEP 3 짧은 대화 연습 발음 / 강세 훈련

A What do normally do for **family holidays**?
B Well, we **get together with our relatives.**
A What do you do when you gather?
B We **cook holiday food** together and **exchange gifts.**

A 명절에 주로 뭐하니?
B 음, 친척들하고 한자리에 모여.
A 모이면 뭐하는데?
B 같이 명절 음식하고 선물 교환하지.

138 휴일 활동

STEP 1 주제어 핵심 단어 학습 발음 / 강세 훈련

가족과 시간을 보내다	spend time with family
친구를 만나다	meet up with one's friends
영화보러 가다	go see a movie
외식하다	eat out at a restaurant
야외로 나가다	go outdoors
야외활동을 하다	do some outdoor activities
소풍을 가다	go on a picnic
자전거를 타다	ride one's bike

STEP 2 짧은 영작 연습 발음 / 강세 훈련

(1) 이번 연휴 때 가족들과 시간을 보낼 거야.

(spend time with family)

I am going to spend time with family during the holidays.

(2) 이번 연휴 때 야외에 나가서 뭘 좀 하고 싶어.

(do some outdoor activities)

I want to do some outdoor activities during the holidays.

(3) 우리 나가서 밥도 먹고 영화도 봤어.

(meet up with friends / eat out at a restaurant)

We met up with my friends and ate out at a restaurant.

STEP 3 짧은 대화 연습 발음 / 강세 훈련

A What did you do yesterday?

B **I met up with my friends and ate out at a restaurant.**

A Did you have fun?

B Yes! I hadn't seen them in a long time.

A 어제 뭐했니?

B 친구들 만나서 외식했어.

A 재미 있었어?

B 응! 친구들 정말 오랜만에 본 거였거든.

139

휴일 변화

STEP 1 주제어 핵심 단어 학습 발음 / 강세 훈련

휴일 트렌드	holiday trends
하루를 추가로 쉬다	take an extra day off
연휴	extended holiday
해외로 나가다	go overseas
해외여행	overseas trip
호캉스를 가다	book a hotel package
집에서 편하게 쉬다	kick back and relax at home
마사지를 받다	get a massage

STEP 2 짧은 영작 연습 발음 / 강세 훈련

(1) 다음 주에 긴 연휴가 있어.

(extended holiday)

We have an extended holiday next week.

(2) 사람들이 요즘 해외여행을 더 자주 가는 편이야.

(do some outdoor activities)

People take overseas trips more often these days.

(3) 어떤 사람들은 그냥 집에서 편이 쉬는 것을 좋아해.

(kick back and relax at home)

Some people just like to kick back and relax at home.

STEP 3 짧은 대화 연습 발음 / 강세 훈련

A What are you doing during the holidays?

B My wife and I booked a hotel package.

A Oh, really?

B Yeah, we're just going to kick back and relax.

A 연휴 때 뭐할 거니?

B 아내하고 호텔 패키지 예약했어.

A 정말?

B 응. 그냥 편하게 쉴까 생각 중이야.

140

휴일 사건사고

STEP 1 주제어 핵심 단어 학습 발음 / 강세 훈련

사고 나다	get into an accident
아프다	get sick
다치다	get hurt
부상당하다	get injured
넘어지다	fall down
멍이 들다	get a bruise
찢어지다	get a cut
체하다	get indigestion
식중독에 걸리다	get food poisoning
~을 두고 오다	leave something behind

STEP 2 짧은 영작 연습 발음 / 강세 훈련

(1) 나 사고가 나서 부상을 당했어.

(get into an accident / get injured)

I got injured because I got into an accident.

(2) 나 넘어져서 무릎에 멍이 들었어.

(get a bruise / fall down)

I fell down and got a bruise.

(3) 나 식중독에 걸려서 정말 고생했어.

(get food poisoning)

I really had a tough time
because I got food poisoning.

STEP 3 짧은 대화 연습 발음 / 강세 훈련

A What happened to your arm?
Did you get hurt?

B I fell down and hurt my arm.

A Oh, no! Did you break it?

B No, I just got a big bruise.

A 팔 어떻게 된 거야? 다쳤어?
B 넘어져서 팔을 다쳤어.
A 아이고! 부러진 거니?
B 아니, 그냥 크게 멍이 들었어.

매일 10분 영어 이현석의

정면돌파 스피킹

www.ebse.co.kr

여가
생활편

Love
사랑

unit 141 ~ unit 145

141

사랑

STEP 1 주제어 핵심 단어 학습 발음 / 강세 훈련

~에게 호감이 있다	have feelings for
사랑에 빠지다	fall in love
~를 사랑하고 있다	be in love with
미친듯이 사랑에 빠지다	be madly in love
~를 엄청 좋아하다	have a crush on
~에게 흠뻑 빠지다	be head over heels for
~에 집착하다	be obsessed with
첫눈에 반한 사랑	love at first sight

STEP 2 짧은 영작 연습 발음 / 강세 훈련

(1) 그들은 결국 사랑에 빠졌다.
(fall in love)
They eventually fell in love.

(2) 나는 고등학교 때 그를 엄청 좋아했다.
(have a crush on)
I had a crush on him when I was in high school.

(3) 내 생각에는 첫눈에 반한 사랑이었던 같아.
(love at first sight)
I think it was love at first sight.

STEP 3 짧은 대화 연습 발음 / 강세 훈련

A I think they **are madly in love.**
B It seems like they are.
A They told me it was **love at first sight.**
B They make a perfect couple, don't you think?

A 저들은 서로 정말 사랑하는 거 같아.
B 그래 보여.
A 첫눈에 사랑에 빠진 거라고 하더라고.
B 둘이 정말 잘 어울려. 안 그래?

142

데이트

STEP 1 주제어 핵심 단어 학습 발음 / 강세 훈련

데이트 / 데이트 상대	date
데이트가 있다	have a date
데이트를 하다	go on a date
~에게 데이트 신청하다	ask someone out on a date
~를 사귀다	date someone
소개팅	blind date
~와 교제하다	go out with someone
~를 만나다	see someone
까다롭게 굴다 / 튕기다	play hard to get

STEP 2 짧은 영작 연습 발음 / 강세 훈련

(1) 나 오늘 저녁에 데이트 있어.

(have a date)

I have a date tonight.

(2) 그 친구에게 데이트 신청해보지 그래?

(ask someone out on a date)

Why don't you ask her out on a date?

(3) 지금 만나고 있는 사람 있어요?

(see someone)

Are you seeing anyone right now?

STEP 3 짧은 대화 연습 발음 / 강세 훈련

A I heard they are going on a date tonight.

B No, she cancelled the date.

A Are you sure?
He was really looking forward to it.

B I think she is playing hard to get.

A 그들이 오늘 데이트를 할거라고 들었어.
B 아니야. 그녀가 데이트를 취소했어.
A 정말? 그 친구가 정말 기대 많이 하고 있었는데.
A 그녀가 까다롭게 굴고 있는 거 같아.

143

연인

STEP 1 주제어 핵심 단어 학습 발음 / 강세 훈련

커플이 되다	be together
커플이다	be a thing
남자친구	boyfriend
여자친구	girlfriend
공개 커플	official couple
공개적으로 사귀다	officially see each other
비밀리에 사귀다	secretly see each other
전남친 / 전여친	ex

STEP 2 짧은 영작 연습 발음 / 강세 훈련

(1) 그들이 커플인지 전혀 몰랐네.

(be a thing)

I have no idea that they were a thing.

(2) 그들은 이제 공개적으로 사귀는 거 같아.

(officially see each other)

I think they are officially seeing each other now.

(3) 전남친과 마주치고 싶지 않아.

(ex)

I don't want to run into my ex.

STEP 3 짧은 대화 연습 발음 / 강세 훈련

A **Are** they **together now**?

B **Yes**, it **seems** like they **are a thing.**

A I had **no clue.**

B Me, **neither**. I **think** they have been **secretly seeing each other** for a **while**.

A 그 친구들 이제 커플인가?
B 응. 사귀는 거처럼 보여.
A 전혀 몰랐네.
B 나도 그래. 한동안 비밀리에 사귀어 온 거 같아.

144

결혼

STEP 1 주제어 핵심 단어 학습 발음 / 강세 훈련

결혼하다	get married
결혼하다	tie the knot
결혼하다	walk down the aisle
시집가다/장가 가다	get hitched
신랑신부	bride and groom
청혼	proposal
청혼하다	pop the big question
결혼식	wedding ceremony
결혼식 하객	wedding guest
신혼여행	honeymoon

STEP 2 짧은 영작 연습 발음 / 강세 훈련

(1) 그들 드디어 결혼하는 구나.

(tie the knot)

They are finally tying the knot.

(2) 남자 친구가 프로포즈 했어?

(pop the big question)

Did you boyfriend pop the big question?

(3) 결혼식 하객들에게 청첩장을 보냈어.

(wedding guest)

We sent out the invitations to the wedding guests.

STEP 3 짧은 대화 연습 발음 / 강세 훈련

A **My boyfriend popped the big question last night!**

B **Wow! Congratulations!**

A **It was so unexpected!**

B **I'm so happy for you!
You guys are finally tying the knot.**

A 내 남자 친구가 어제 저녁에 프로포즈 했어.
B 우와! 축하해!
A 전혀 예상 못 했어.
B 너무 잘 됐다! 너희들 드디어 결혼 하는구나!

145

이별

STEP 1 주제어 핵심 단어 학습 발음 / 강세 훈련

헤어지다	break up
이별	breakup
마음 아픈	painful
차다	dump someone
차이다	be dumped by someone
상처를 입히다	break one's heart
상처를 받다	be heart-broken
잊고 극복하다	get over someone
새롭게 시작하다	move on

STEP 2 짧은 영작 연습 발음 / 강세 훈련

(1) 그들이 최근에 헤어졌다고 들었어.
(break up)
I heard they broke up recently.

(2) 나는 마음 아픈 이별을 했어.
(painful breakup)
I went through a painful breakup.

(3) 그녀가 그에게 큰 상처를 줬어.
(break one's heart)
She broke his heart.

STEP 3 짧은 대화 연습 발음 / 강세 훈련

A He went through a **painful breakup** last year.
B Yeah, I know that he was **heart-broken**.
A I don't think he has **gotten over her** yet.
B Really? It's been over a year now.

A 그 친구가 작년에 마음 아픈 이별을 했어.
B 응. 상처를 크게 받았지.
A 아직 그녀를 잊지 못 한 거 같아.
B 정말? 이제 일년이라는 시간이 지났는데.

여가 생활편

Pets
반려동물

unit 146 ~ unit 150

146

반려동물 인구

STEP 1 주제어 핵심 단어 학습 발음 / 강세 훈련

반려동물을 기르다	have a pet
반려동물 주인	pet owner
반려동물을 기르는 가구	household with pets
반려동물 용품점	pet store
개 용품	dog supplies
고양이 용품	cat supplies
사랑과 관심	love and care
책임감	responsibility
의지	commitment

STEP 2 짧은 영작 연습 발음 / 강세 훈련

(1) 반려동물을 기르는 가정이 이제 많다.
(household with pets)
There are many households with pets now.

(2) 반려동물 용품점들도 주변에 정말 많이 있다.
(pet store)
There are pet stores all over the place.

(3) 반려동물을 기르는 것은 큰 책임과 의지가 필요하다.
(responsibility / commitment)
Having a pet is a big responsibility and commitment.

STEP 3 짧은 대화 연습 발음 / 강세 훈련

A There are **many households with pets** now.
B That's right. My neighbors all have pets.
A That's why there are **pet stores** all over the place.
B Uh-huh. People have to get **dog supplies or cat supplies.**

A 반려동물을 기르는 가정이 이제 정말 많아.
B 맞아. 우리 이웃들도 전부 동물을 키워.
A 그래서 사방에 반려동물 용품점들이 생긴 거 같아.
B 응. 사람들이 개 용품, 고양이 용품을 사야 하니까.

147

개

STEP 1 주제어 핵심 단어 학습 발음 / 강세 훈련

개를 기르다	have a dog
개를 입양하다	adopt a dog
강아지	puppy
개를 산책시키다	walk one's dog
개목걸이 / 목줄	collar / leash
목욕시키다	give one's a dog a bath
개 사료 / 개 간식	dog food / dog biscuit
배변 훈련을 시키다	potty train
용변 패드	pee pad
미용 관리를 받다	get one's dog groomed

STEP 2 짧은 영작 연습 발음 / 강세 훈련

(1) 나는 개를 최소 하루에 한번은 산책 시킨다.
(walk one's dog)
I walk my dog at least once a day.

(2) 개를 밖으로 데리고 나갈 때는 항상 목줄을 해야 한다.
(leash)
You always need to have your dog on a leash when you take him out.

(3) 오늘 우리 개 미용 관리를 받았어.
(get one's dog groomed)
I get my dog groomed today.

STEP 3 짧은 대화 연습 발음 / 강세 훈련

A How often do you **take your dog out**?
B I **walk my dog** at least once a day.
A Are you doing that today as well?
B Yes, I'm also **getting him groomed** today.

A 개를 얼마나 자주 데리고 나가니?
B 최소 하루에 한번은 산책 시켜.
A 오늘도 할 거니?
B 응. 오늘 미용 관리도 받게 하려고.

148

고양이

STEP 1 주제어 핵심 단어 학습 발음 / 강세 훈련

고양이를 기르다	have a cat
새끼 고양이	kitten
종	breed
암컷인지 수컷인지	he or she / male or female
고양이 사료	cat food
고양이 밥주다	feed one's cat
고양이 타워	cat tower
고양이 장난감	cat toy
고양이 화장실	litter box
발톱을 깎아주다	clip one's nails

STEP 2 짧은 영작 연습 발음 / 강세 훈련

(1) 우리 고양이들은 새끼 때 입양을 했어.
(kitten)
I adopted my cats when they were kittens.

(2) 암컷이에요, 수컷이에요?
(he or she)
Is it a he or a she?

(3) 고양이 밥주고, 화장실 청소해줘야 해.
(feed one's cat / litter box)
I need to feed my cat and clean her litter box.

STEP 3 짧은 대화 연습 발음 / 강세 훈련

A I have to go home now.
B But it's only 9pm.
Why don't you stay a little longer?
A I have to go **feed my cat**.
She's been starving all day.
I also have to **clean her litter box**.
B Oh, I see. Off you go then!

A 나 이제 집에 가야 돼.
B 밤 9시 밖에 안 되었는데. 조금만 더 있다 가지 그래?
A 고양이 밥 줘야 돼. 하루 종일 굶고 있어.
화장실도 청소해줘야 하고.
B 아, 그렇구나. 어서 가 그럼.

149 동물병원

STEP 1 주제어 핵심 단어 학습 발음 / 강세 훈련

수의사	vet / veterinarian
동물병원에 데려가다	take one's dog to the vet
아프다	get sick
피부병이 생기다	have a skin condition
예방접종을 받다	get a vaccination
심장사상충 약	heartworm medication
중성화 수술을 시키다	neuter
이름표를 달다	get a name tag
등록하다	register

STEP 2 짧은 영작 연습 발음 / 강세 훈련

(1) 개를 동물병원에 데리고 가야 해.
(take one's dog to the vet)
I need to take my dog to the vet.

(2) 우리 고양이 오늘 예방접종 맞아야 해.
(get a vaccination)
My cat needs to get a vaccination today.

(3) 고양이를 어렸을 때 중성화 수술해줬어.
(neuter)
I had my cat neutered when she was young.

STEP 3 짧은 대화 연습 발음 / 강세 훈련

A I need to take my dog to the vet.
B Is he sick?
A No, he needs to get his vaccination.
B I see. Is the vet close by?

A 오늘 개를 동물병원에 데리고 가야 해.
B 개가 어디 아프니?
A 아니, 예방접종 맞아야 돼서.
B 그렇구나. 동물병원이 가까운데 있니?

150

동물보호

STEP 1 주제어 핵심 단어 학습 발음 / 강세 훈련

동물권리	animal rights
동물보호법	animal protection law
반려동물을 유기하다	abandon pets
유기동물	homeless animals
유기견	stray dogs
유기묘	stray cats
동물보호소	animal shelter
안락사시키다	put to sleep

STEP 2 짧은 영작 연습 발음 / 강세 훈련

(1) 조금 더 강력한 동물보호법이 있어야 할 거 같아.
(animal protection law)
I think we need a stronger animal protection law.

(2) 어떤 사람들은 동물을 유기하는 경우가 있다.
(abandon pets)
Some people abandon their pets.

(3) 많은 반려동물들이 동물보호소에서 새 주인을 기다리고 있다.
(animal shelter)
Many pets are waiting for their new owners at animal shelters.

STEP 3 짧은 대화 연습 발음 / 강세 훈련

A There are so many **homeless animals.**

B I know. That's because many people **abandon their pets.**

A I think it's so sad.

B Many pets are waiting for their new owners at **animal shelters.**

A 유기동물이 정말 많아.
B 알아. 많은 사람들이 반려동물을 유기해서 그래.
A 너무 슬픈 거 같아.
B 많은 반려동물들이 동물 보호소에서 새 주인을 기다리고 있어.

부록

잘 알아듣는 강세 연습

강세를 콕콕 채워넣기

unit 66. 영화 장르

나는 공포영화는 별로 안 좋아해.

I am ________ a ________ fan of ____rror movies.

unit 67. 영화관

그 영화 다음 상영시간이 몇 시니?

________ is the ________ showing for ________ movie?

unit 68. 영화 감상

그 영화 예고편 봤는데, 정말 보고 싶어

I _____ched the _______er for that ____vie,

and I _____ly want to _______ it.

unit 69. 영화 흥행

그 영화는 조기 종영 되었어.

The ________ was be taken ______ _____ly from the theaters.

unit 70. 영화 배우

너 가장 좋아하는 영화 배우가 누구니?

________ is your ____vorite ____vie star?

unit 71. 음악 취향

나는 힙합 음악을 정말 좋아해요.

I am ______ly into ______-hop music.

unit 72. 좋아하는 가수

그 사람은 정말 대단한 가수인 거 같아.

I ________ he is an in_______dible singer.

unit 73. 음악을 듣는 습관

나는 이제 음악을 어디서든 들을 수 있다.

I can ______ ____sten to ____sic wher______ I am.

unit 74. 음악 기기

선이 꼬이지 않아서 좋다.

I ______ it because the ______ do ______ get ______gled ____.

unit 75. K-POP

그들의 신곡은 여러 음악 차트 1위를 기록했다.

Their ______ song _____ No.1 on the ____sic charts.

unit 76. 방송 취향

우리 아이들은 만화영화를 매일 본다.

My ________ren watch car________ __very day.

unit 77. 방송 시청

나는 저녁 먹을 때 TV 틀어 놓는 것을 좋아해.

I _______ to _______ the T__ _____ when I'm ____ving dinner.

unit 78. 뉴스 방송

이제는 뉴스를 실시간으로 접할 수 있다.

We can _______ the _______ (in) _______ time now.

unit 79. 방송 변화

TV 방송은 정말 몰라보게 발전해 왔다.

T___ _______grams have _______ a _______ way.

unit 80. 인터넷 방송

나는 넷플릭스 정기구독하고 있어.

I _______ a sub_______tion on _______flix.

unit 81. 경기 관람

분위기가 달아 올랐다.

The ________ _______ heated _____.

unit 82. 야구

우리 팀이 5회초에 2득점을 했다.

Our ________ scored ________ runs in the ________ of 5th inning.

unit 83. 축구

우리는 전반에 2골을 넣었다.

We ______red ________ goals in the ___________ half.

unit 84. 농구

그는 3쿼터에만 12점을 넣었어.

He ______red ______ points in the _________ quarter a__________.

unit 85. 테니스

나는 단식보다는 복식 경기를 더 자주 해.

I ________ ______bles in______ of ______gles ________ often.

unit 86. 소셜미디어 활동

나는 그 게시물을 내 페이지에 공유했어.

I re______ed that ________ing on my ________.

unit 87. 페이스북

너 페이스북 하니?

________ you on ________book?

unit 88. 인스타그램

그 게시물에 너 태그 했어.

I ________ged you on the ________ing.

unit 89. 트위터

그 사람 팔로우 취소 해야 할 거 같아.

I __________ I should un_______ow him.

unit 90. 유튜브

그 영상은 백만이 넘는 조회수를 기록했다.

The ______ got ______ than a ______ion views.

unit 91. 모바일 게임

요즘 가장 인기 있는 모바일 게임이 뭐니?

______ is the ______test ______bile game ________ days?

unit 92. 게임 설치

그 게임 휴대폰에 지금 설치했어.

I in______ed that ______ on my ________.

unit 93. 게임 중독

나 이 게임에 중독된 거 같아.

I ________ I am a______ted to this ________.

unit 94. 프로게이머

프로게이머들은 엄청난 반사신경을 가지고 있다.

Pro________onal gamers have a ______zing ______flexes.

unit 95. 보드 게임

너 주사위 두 번 던져야 해.

You ________ to ________ the ________ twice.

unit 96. 휴가 신청

나 며칠 휴가 낼 생각이야.

I'm ________ing of ___king a ______ days ______.

unit 97. 휴가 계획

호텔 예약하고 항공권 구매했어.

I _______ed a ho_____ and _____ a _________ ticket.

unit 98. 휴가 비용

나 바가지 쓴 거 같아.

I __________ I _______ ripped _______.

unit 99. 휴가 에피소드

공항에서 몇 차례나 길을 잃었어.

I _______ lost ____veral times at the _____port.

unit 100. 집에서 보내는 휴가

집에서 밀린 잠이나 조금 자고 싶어.

I _______ want to catch _____ on some __________.

unit 101. 인터넷 쇼핑몰

인터넷 쇼핑 얼마나 자주 하니?

_______ often do you _______ online?

unit 102. 인터넷 결제

지금 사면 10% 할인을 받을 수 있어.

You can _____ 10 pe_______ off if you _______ it _______.

unit 103. 인터넷 교환/환불

교환할 거니, 아니면 환불할 거니?

Are you _____ing to _____ an ex_______ge or _____ a _____fund?

unit 104. 인터넷 쇼핑 장단점

허위 광고에 속지 않게 조심해.

Be ______ful ______ to fall for ______se ads.

unit 105. 중고품 거래

그거 절반 가격에 살 수 있어.

You can ________ it at ________ the __________.

unit 106. 건강 유지

나는 규칙적으로 운동을 하려고 노력해.

I ________ to work ________ on a _____gular _____sis.

unit 107. 질병 예방

운동은 여러 질병과 만성질환을 예방해준다.

_____ercising pre________ various _____nesses and _________nic di_______ses.

unit 108. 유산소 운동

유산소 운동을 매일 한 시간씩 하고 있어.

I _____ some _____dio for an ________ ___very day.

unit 109. 근력 운동

나 복근 운동을 많이 하고 있어.

I'm ________ing a ______ on my ______.

unit 110. 헬스/요가

요즘 요가 배우는 사람들이 정말 많아.

There are __________ people who _________ ____ga classes these days.

unit 111. 학창 시절 친구

그 친구는 학창시절 친구야.

She is a _____iend _________ from ___________.

unit 112. 고마운 친구

그 친구는 나가 하는 일을 항상 지지해줘.

She is _______ sup_____tive of _______ I _____.

unit 113. 친구 연락

너희들 서로 연락하고 지내니?

Do you _________ _________ in __________?

unit 114. 친구 모임

나 어제 친구들 모임이 있었어.

I _________ a ______thering with my _______ends _________terday.

unit 115. 싸움/화해

나 그 친구하고 크게 싸웠어.

I _________ a _________ fight with him.

unit 116. 음식점 종류

내가 정말 좋아하는 베트남 음식점이 있어.

We _______ had _______ner at a _____cal ____staurant.

unit 117. 음식점 메뉴

메인 요리가 나오기 전에 에피타이저가 나왔어.

They ________ght us an _____petizer before the _________ dish.

unit 118. 음식점 계산

우리 나눠서 계산할까요?

Should we __________ the _______?

unit 119. 음식점 검색

음식점 검색해보자.

Let's _______ an ______line search for a _________

to _______.

unit 120. 음식 배달/테이크아웃

우리 오늘 그냥 시켜 먹는 것이 어떠니?

_______ don't we _________ order ____ today?

unit 121. 커피숍 종류

내가 자주 가는 동네 카페가 있어요.

There is a _____cal ca______ I go to _____ten.

unit 122. 커피숍 메뉴

나는 항상 아메리카노만 주문해.

I _____ways _____der an _____meri_____no.

unit 123. 커피숍 위치

요즘에는 사방에 커피숍들이 있는 거 같아.

_____fee shops are _____ over the _______ _______

days.

unit 124. 커피숍 주문

뭐 시킬지 정했니?

Have you de_____ed _______ to _____?

unit 125. 커피숍 가격

일부 커피숍 음료 가격이 너무 비싼 거 같아.

I ________ drinks at ________ ______fee shops are _______priced.

unit 126. 술 종류

병맥주 좋아하세요, 생맥주 좋아하세요?

Do you _______ ________ beer or ________ beer?

unit 127. 술안주

치킨은 맥주와 정말 잘 어울린다.

_____ed chicken ______lly goes _______ with _______.

unit 128. 술집

나 동네 술집 한 군데에 단골이야.

I'm a _____gular at a _____cal bar.

unit 129. 과음

나는 취해서 창피한 실수를 했어.

I ________ an em______assing mis________ because I was __________.

unit 130. 숙취

나 숙취가 정말 심해.

I ________ a _____rrible _________over.

unit 131. 모임 종류

이번 주말에 가족 모임이 있어요.

I ________ a ________ly gathering ________ weekend.

unit 132. 모임 계획

나는 모임을 자주 주선하는 편이야.

I _____ganize _____therings _________ often.

unit 133. 모임 비용

우리 이번 모임 비용은 어떻게 처리할꺼니?

_______ are we ____ing to ____ver the _________

for the _____thering?

unit 134. 모임 빈도

우리는 그냥 번개를 해서 만나는 경우가 많아.

We _________ get to_____ther _______domly.

unit 135. 모임 추억

정말 기억에 남는 모임이었어.

It was a _________ _____morable _____thering.

unit 136. 공휴일

현충일에 뭐 할 거니?

_________ are you ____ing on Me_____rial Day?

unit 137. 명절

한국에는 큰 명절이 두 개가 있다.

There are ________ _____mily holidays in ______ea.

unit 138. 휴일 활동

이번 연휴 때 가족들과 시간을 보낼 거야.

I am ____ing to __________ time with _____mily

during the _____lidays.

unit 139. 휴일 변화

다음 주에 긴 연휴가 있어.

We ______ an ex________ed _____liday ______ week.

unit 140. 휴일 사건사고

나 넘어져서 무릎에 멍이 들었어.

I fell ________ and ______ a ________.

unit 141. 사랑

그들은 결국 사랑에 빠졌다.

They e________tually ________ in ________.

unit 142. 데이트

그 친구에게 데이트 신청해보지 그래?

______ don't you ______ her ______ on a ______?

unit 143. 연인

전남친과 마주치고 싶지 않아.

I ________ want to ________ into my ______.

unit 144. 결혼

결혼식 하객들에게 청첩장을 보냈어.

We sent ________ the _____vi_____tions to the ______ding guests.

unit 145. 이별

나는 마음 아픈 이별을 했어.

I _______ through a _______ful _________up.

unit 146. 반려동물 인구

반려동물을 기르는 것은 큰 책임과 의지가 필요하다.

_____ving a _____ is a _____ res_____si_____lity and com_____tment.

unit 147. 개

나는 개를 최소 하루에 한번은 산책 시킨다.

I _____ my _____ at _____ _____ a _____.

unit 148. 고양이

암컷이에요, 수컷이에요?.

Is it a _____ or a _____?

unit 149. 동물병원

개를 동물병원에 데리고 가야 해.

I _____ to _____ my _____ to the _____.

unit 150. 동물보호

조금 더 강력한 동물보호법이 있어야 할 거 같아.

I _____ we _____ a _____er animal pro_____tion law.